EuroManagers
& Martians

Richard Hill

VISIT US ON INTERNET - OUR ADDRESS :

Netscape - [Understanding

File   Edit   View   Go   Bookmarks   Options   Directory

Back   Forward   Home   Reload   Images   Open   Print   Find   Stop

Location: http://www.understanding-europe.com

Published by Europublic SA/NV,
Avenue Winston Churchill 11 (box 21),   B-1180 Brussels.
Tel: + 32 2 343 77 26   Fax. +32 2 343 93 30

Illustrations: Bob Pater
Cover design : Marc Segond

1st edition May 1994.
2nd edition September 1998.

Printed in Belgium. Edition et Imprimerie, Brussels.
D/1998/6421/1   ISBN 90-74440-13-4

I dedicate this book to Hayao Nakamura, who unwittingly sowed the seed, and owe acknowledgements to many more people than I could name - and who in any case choose to remain anonymous. They shared their experience with me, sharpened my perception, and gave me encouragement. My thanks to them all.

Chapter 1

Introduction

This book, you may notice, is dedicated to a Japanese I have not been privileged to meet. I first heard about him in a sidebar of the *International Herald Tribune*. Mr Nakamura was at the time (May 1993) the manager of ILVA, the Italian state-owned postwar Mezzogiorno steel company - the kind of organisation that challenges the imagination of even the most sophisticated European.

Maybe that was why the Italian government, already enmeshed in the web of *Tangentopoli*, decided to call on the services of a Japanese - a very able one - to sort out the mess. Admittedly, he was a long-time resident of Italy, but had never felt comfortable "doing as the Romans do".

Later - and significantly no longer as manager but as a consultant to ILVA - he explained the ILVA debacle with this memorable thought: "Human stupidity is to blame. The Italians are more human and therefore more stupid. They just sat down and never planned for the future."

So, seen from even a Japanese standpoint, you can explain the European economic dilemma in cultural terms - and that's what this book is all about.

And Mr Nakamura? Well, the only thanks he got for his efforts - which were sufficiently un-Italian to look alien - was that the Italians dubbed him "the Martian".

Both EuroManagers and Martians are much talked-about but as yet unverified forms of life, despite frequent sightings. This book looks at the 'culturo-managerial' stock available for the creation of a EuroManager breed, and in its conclusion examines breeding methods and the chances of success.

•••

In an earlier book[1] I set out to explain the value systems and behavioural traits of the various cultures that make up Europe. I prefer to talk about 'cultures' rather than 'countries' because the nation states as we inherited them represent a rather messy interpretation of the European reality.

In that book, I devoted a chapter to the Europeans in business, examining the way cultures affect values and behaviour in an organisational environment.

Although there are some big organisations that still believe corporate cultures and mission statements can erase individual personality, it should by now be pretty self-evident that, unless they are superhuman, people don't 'leave themselves at home' when they go to work.

Yet the insights one gains from the study of human nature can be augmented by examining behaviour in the workplace and that is what this book intends to do. I am looking at how individual cultures impact in different ways on professional preferences and performance, whether in business, industry, the administrations, the professions or academia. In every case, the individual is to some extent constrained by his occupational environment.

The importance of understanding how cultures influence the way people behave in business - already a burgeoning area of endeavour - is enhanced by current changes in management thinking, where processes like downsizing and company re-engineering put the spotlight firmly on individual behaviour and potential.

In the closing chapter of this book I examine the viability of creating a EuroManager species - someone who, on the one hand, has to try to be 'all things to all men' while, on the other, providing the entrepreneurial spark essential to any business in a rapidly changing world.

Reactions to my earlier book have been a valuable and greatly appreciated source of input. One of the things I have learned in the process - and which is worth mentioning right at the outset - is that while, in my opinion, social (or national) cultures will always win out against corporate cultures, there is yet another set of cultures that can prove equally strong if not stronger - and that is professional cultures. Lawyers tend to behave the same everywhere. The same goes for accountants, and so on. But more of that later...

Chapter 2

The Ground Rules

A rguments rage about the correct and proper way of tackling the issue of the differences between cultures (which in many cases, but not always, means nationalities).

Some academics have searched for scientifically verifiable differences, originally physical, nowadays psychological. History records a variety of approaches. Aristotle maintained that climate was a determinant of human behaviour: people in cold climes were brave but stupid, people from the warmer parts of the world were less brave but intelligent - and the Greeks, who were in the middle, were (guess what?) both brave **and** intelligent.

Later, much later, came the phrenologists who thought you could determine a person's character by the shape of his head and, even later, the geneticists who for a while espoused the deplorable race psychology of the early 20th century.

Fortunately, these fads are now behind us. Today the argument is between those who favour a statistical approach (whether it is based on the raw data itself or on the 'general public's' perception of such things) and those who prefer observation. Both schools are, of course, right.

By inclination I favour the second school - which happens to be convenient as by temperament I am an 'observationist', to coin a word. In support I can offer the credo of John Kotter, professor of leadership and corporate culture at the Harvard Business School, who states that "real progress in the study of managerial work relies on the use of unstructured observation methods."

Yet the 'non-observationists' (the simplest way of describing those of another conviction) bring as much to the understanding of human cultures as the 'observationists' do. They do **not** preclude the value of direct observation, they prefer to use it to confirm their scientific conclusions rather than the other way round.

The five pillars...

Three professional researchers stand out as pioneers in the use of scientific methods to throw light into the opaque depths of human cultural mindsets. They, curiously, all bear names beginning with an 'H': Hofstede, Hoppe and Hall. The first of these is a Dutch national, the second a German who has made his home in the United States, and the third an American (let me take this opportunity to acknowledge the US contribution to a better understanding of ourselves, Europeans).

Professor Geert Hofstede, founder of the Institute for Research on Intercultural Cooperation (IRIC) in Maastricht, is the architect of the five 'pillars' or parameters - he uses the word dimensions - which underpin any serious investigation into cultural traits and differences. Others have introduced parallel dimensions, or added glosses to his work, but Hofstede has provided us with the essential tools for cultural understanding. There is rarely need to look further - although, in a spirit of fairness, Michael Hoppe insists I acknowledge the pioneering work of Harry Triandis and Shalom H Schwartz.

What precisely do we mean by 'culture'? In his latest book[2], Hofstede captures the concept graphically in the phrase 'software of the mind'. Elaborating in his introduction he says: "The sources of one's mental programs lie within the social environments in which one grew up and collected one's life experiences. The programming starts within the family; it continues within the neighborhood, at school, in youth groups, at the work place, and in the living community." In other words, also his, culture is the "collective programming of the mind."

Hofstede's study of employee value systems is based on 117,000 questionnaires he and his staff analysed when he was working as a researcher with the central personnel department of IBM. This pioneering study, dubbed 'Project Hermes', was conducted among 50 different occupational groups of employees in the late-1960s and early-70s, and covered 40 countries both in Europe and outside. It was subsequently extended and updated by further studies undertaken in the late-70s and early-80s.

Hofstede categorised national cultures in terms of these four dimensions: (1) **individualism** versus **collectivism**, (2) **large power distance** versus **small power distance**, (3) **strong uncertainty avoidance** versus **weak uncertainty avoidance** and (4) **masculinity** versus **femininity**.

14

These dimensions were defined by Hofstede in the following ways:

(1)   individualism versus collectivism reflects the degree to which people define themselves by the group or organisation to which they belong, and corresponds to a large extent to national wealth. The northern European countries lie at the 'individualistic' end of the scale with, perhaps surprisingly, Austria and, not so surprisingly at the time, Spain trailing behind and Portugal even further back.

(2)   power distance describes a society's response to inequality in power among its members. This dimension is low in the northern European countries of Scandinavia, the UK and Germany (also, again rather surprisingly, Austria) and relatively high in France, Belgium, Italy, Spain, Portugal and Greece.

(3)   uncertainty avoidance is the extent to which a society feels threatened by unsure and ambiguous situations and consequently searches for statutory structures. This dimension is lowest in Denmark, Sweden, the UK and Ireland, and particularly high in Belgium, France, Germany, Austria, Switzerland and Finland, as well as in the high power distance countries of the Mediterranean.

(4)   masculinity versus femininity represents opposing poles in social attitudes (showing off, 'performing', achieving, 'big is beautiful' *versus* putting personal relationships, respect for quality of life etc, before material goods). On this dimension the German-speaking countries rate as relatively 'masculine' and The Netherlands and Scandinavia as 'feminine'. The record in the case of the Mediterranean countries is mixed: Italy and Greece turn out to be very 'masculine' while Spain, contrary to the macho folklore, proves to be 'feminine'.

Since defining these dimensions - which are applicable in varying degrees to all European cultures - Geert Hofstede together with Michael Bond, now Professor of Psychology at the Chinese University of Hong Kong, identified another that particularly sets off Europeans against the cultures of other continents: **short-term orientation** versus **long-term orientation**. Witness the difference in the attitudes to time between the Europeans (or Americans) on the one hand and the Japanese (or Arabs) on the other.

Values of Hofstede's Four Dimensions - Europe

Country	Individualism vs Collectivism	Power Distance	Uncertainty Avoidance	Masculinity vs Femininity
Austria	55	11	70	79
Belgium	75	65	94	54
Denmark	74	18	23	16
Finland	63	33	59	26
France	71	68	86	43
West Germany	67	35	65	66
Greece	35	60	112	57
Ireland	70	28	35	68
Italy	76	50	75	70
Netherlands	80	38	53	14
Norway	69	31	50	8
Portugal	27	63	104	31
Spain	51	57	86	42
Sweden	71	31	29	5
Switzerland	68	34	58	70
United Kingdom	89	35	35	66

Source: *Culture's Consequences*, Sage Publications, 1980, page 315. Copyright: Prof. Geert Hofstede.

Anyone who has spent some time travelling around Europe will already have mentally logged some clear examples of dimensions (1) individualism v collectivism and (4) masculinity v femininity, also of varying attitudes towards time (and I am not thinking of the fact that status-conscious Latins deliberately turn up late for appointments...).

In fact the country ratings obtained by the Hermes study on Hofstede's four dimensions largely parallel specific social phenomena which one might logically expect to be associated with such dimensions.

As Hoppe pointed out in his later study (see below): "Large power distance positively correlated with high degrees of income inequality, the age of executives, internal political violence, and conformity. Highly significant positive correlations also existed between strong uncertainty avoidance and such indicators as the requirement to carry I.D. cards, neuroticism, or a high number of civil servants with a law degree. Individualism correlated significantly with national wealth, however, not when poor and affluent countries were analyzed separately. Highly positive correlations were also observed between individualism and civic competence and openness (vs. secrecy), respectively. An illustration of a country-level relationship with masculinity was the observation that countries high on masculinity spent less of their national wealth on international development assistance than those which scored lower on that dimension."

For me the most revealing of Hofstede's dimensions are (2) power distance and particularly (3) uncertainty avoidance. The latter is the least easily comprehensible on first acquaintance but, over time, it becomes highly illuminating - throwing light into corners of national cultures that would otherwise go unnoticed.

Uncertainty avoidance has little to do with risk avoidance, although the two are obviously related. It is perhaps best illustrated by the fact that, as Hofstede points out, the Germans have a law in their constitution to cope with the eventuality that none of the other laws work (the *Notstandsgesetz*), while the British do not even have a written constitution.

In fact, strong uncertainty avoidance is clearly a mindset, or form of mental programming, which is **reinforced** by the existence of a structured statutory environment.

The reverse of the medal, of course, is that weak uncertainty avoidance cultures are allergic to such constraints. André Laurent, a French researcher and consultant, notes that the Swedes and Dutch are far less comfortable with precisely defined roles than are the Germans, French, Belgians and Swiss. That goes for the British too!

The ultimate explanation of these striking differences is historical and worth putting into a nutshell: the origins of

Geert Hofstede describes reactions to a case study presented by Professor James Stevens to the students of INSEAD and involving a conflict between two company departments.

The responses, which were more or less consistent by nationality, are indicative of general attitudes: "The French in majority referred the problem to the next higher authority level [curiously, a Frenchman working in a UK company made the same observation of the British!]. The Germans suggested the setting of rules to resolve such problems in the future. The British wanted to improve communications between the two department heads, perhaps by some kind of human relations training."

From his work with INSEAD students, James Stevens concluded that "the dominant underlying model of an organisation for the **French** was a pyramid, a hierarchical structure held together by the unity of command (larger power distance) as well as by rules (strong uncertainty avoidance). The model for the **Germans** was a well-oiled machine; the exercise of personal command was largely unnecessary because the rules settled everything (strong uncertainty avoidance, but smaller power distance). The model for the **British** was a village market: no decisive hierarchy, flexible rules, and a resolution of problems by negotiating (small power distance and weak uncertainty avoidance)."

Hofstede also describes reactions to an exercise where student groups of different nationalities worked against the clock to find a solution to a common organisational problem. Where the French response was "did we win?", the Germans asked "did we produce the right solution?" and the British merely commented "very interesting".

strong uncertainty avoidance lie in the intensive codification of the laws of the Roman Empire, extended to Germany beyond the *limes* through the efforts of Charlemagne and his successors in the centuries that followed. Essentially this explains why the Nordic peoples and the people of the British Isles (some of whom were late arrivals in the Roman Empire, but kept well clear of Charlemagne and Napoleon), register such weak uncertainty avoidance compared with the rest.

Michael Hoppe, currently on the staff of the Center for Creative Leadership in Greensboro, North Carolina, had the opportunity to verify the 'construct validity' of Hofstede's original four dimensions after working as an assistant director of the Salzburg Seminar, a high-level forum for multicultural and interdisciplinary dialogue. 1,544 valid responses from seminar alumni from 19 countries, most of them European, provided the findings revealed in a Ph.D. study[3] published in 1990.

Hoppe's sample differed from Hofstede's in being more select, both in terms of numbers and status. While Hofstede's respondents were primarily male, socio-economically middle-class, managers, professionals, and technical or clerical employees, Hoppe's were the "elite of their respective societies", highly educated and from a wide range of educational, occupational and organisational backgrounds, about 11 per cent of them self-employed.

Yet Hoppe's findings, in his own words, "significantly supported the usefulness of Geert Hofstede's dimensions for describing cultural differences among countries." Country scores for power distance, uncertainty avoidance, individualism and masculinity correlated significantly with those from Hofstede's study, though for masculinity only after Sweden was excluded from the analysis (the demographic pattern of the Swedish sample proved to be untypical).

As Hoppe says in the conclusions to his study, "a sample of countries whose respondents belong to the elite of their respective societies and who represent a wide range of occupations and employers produced results similar to those of Hofstede's sample of countries, whose respondents were primarily middle-class and came from a single private-sector company." If the contents of his questionnaire had been even more closely attuned to the socio-demographic profile of his sample (rather than reflecting Hofstede's approach), the results would have been even closer.

... and Bubbles of Space

Dr Edward T Hall[4], an American anthropologist, analysed national traits in terms of two parameters, one relating to social organisation (**high context** versus **low context**), the other to attitudes towards time (**polychronic** versus **monochronic**). He offered the following definition of culture, complementing Hofstede's software analogy: "Culture is a system for creating sending, storing and processing information. We analyse the culture to determine how it operates and what its messages mean."

Basically Dr Hall identified Latins (the Italians, Spanish, Portuguese and French, in case there's any doubt) as 'high context' people "who have extensive information networks

---

An executive interviewed for the Andersen Consulting study, 'Doing Business in the New Europe', cited three distinctive dialectical approaches adopted by Europeans in reasoning and negotiating:

1. *The Teutonic (Germanic/Nordic/Central European)*, highly legalistic, beginning with the conclusion, proceeding to the supporting points and returning to the conclusion.

2. *The Romantic (French/Mediterranean/S-E European)*, highly formalistic or Aristotelian/Cartesian, beginning with an introduction (usually theoretical) to the argument, proceeding to at least two and probably three sub-points, each of these having two or three supporting points, and concluding with an 'ergo' or inescapable conclusion.

3. *The Anglo-Saxon (British) Mode*, largely inferential, beginning with concrete or pragmatic observations and proceeding directly to a 'logically inferred' conclusion.

among family, friends, colleagues and clients and are involved in close relationships... As a result, they do not require much contexting (in-depth, background information) because they keep themselves informed about everything." They are interactive in both their personal and professional behaviour patterns.

By comparison, 'low context' Germanics (the Germans, Dutch and Nordics) are by no means so well served by informal networks and need more information to feel comfortable in a situation and arrive at a rational decision. Their approach to life generally is highly segmented and compartmentalised (Hall uses the phrase '**screen-dependent**').

Of course these hold-all concepts of Latins and Germanics are fine as far as they go, but do not properly accommodate the Anglo-Saxons, the Belgians and the Austrians (who in many respects are more Latin than Germanic in behaviour, if not genes). The definitions also fly in the face of ethnic reality: Luigi Barzini[5] asserts that nearly 50 per cent of French nationals have Germanic genes!

The second dimension examined by Edward Hall is peoples' attitude towards, and their **use** of, time. He describes those cultures that tend to do more than one thing at a time as **polychronic** and those that do one thing after another as **monochronic**. The correlation between 'high context' and 'polychronic' and between 'low context' and 'monochronic' is striking.

Polychronic Latins are culturally adept at doing a number of things at the same time and in any order that pleases them at that moment. Monochronic Germanics prefer to do one thing at a time and in a predetermined order. This makes the Germanics **schedule-dependent** and the Latins **schedule-independent** (a polite way of saying that they're often late!).

Coming back to the screen-dependent factor, an extension of Dr Hall's theories is that we all, mostly without knowing it, work within a self-defined territory, what sociologists call 'the intimate zone'. "In low context northern European cultures," he says, "each person has around him an invisible **bubble of space** which expands and contracts depending on his relationship to others, his emotional state, his cultural background and the activity he is performing."

The Germans, who are particularly screen-dependent, reinforce the bubble by resorting, in some cases, to double doors in offices - and also by an almost aggressive protectiveness when defending their rights to tables in public restaurants and bathing towels on Mediterranean beaches. The Dutch, too, still tend to keep their office doors closed, much more so than their neighbours to the north and west.

The 'bubble of space' phenomenon is also evident in the behaviour of Germanics in two other situations. The first is the lift, or elevator, where most people look up, down or directly ahead - unless there's a pair of eyes there. The second is the queue, surprisingly a French invention which was taken over in the last century by the British, possibly encouraged by exaggerated ideas about the importance of time - something that Latins, if not necessarily the French, treat much more casually. But I would not go so far as to suggest, as some people have done, that 'bubble of space' criteria prompt Germanic peoples to queue where Latins do not. Norwegians, whose impatience can often get the better of them, hate to stand in line and wait...

Generally the high context Latins, as well as many of the Slavs, like close contact and are much more sensorially involved with each other than the relatively contact-shy people of northern Europe (which does not prevent the average, autocratic Latin manager from keeping his office door firmly closed!).

It is dangerous, however, to assume that a community, just because it qualifies as Latin or Germanic, will behave in a particular way. As Max Messmer says in his book *Staffing Europe*[6]: "Geographic proximity does not ensure common customs. For instance, while Spain and Portugal occupy the Iberian Peninsula together, Spaniards tend to be more demonstrative in public; friendly embrace during a greeting is acceptable, if not common. The Portuguese, on the other hand, are more reserved, and such physical contact is often unwelcomed."

The Spanish proclivity is shared by the Greeks, in the opinion of another American professor, W H McNeil[7], who observes that "small Greek children maintain close physical intimacy - touching each other, holding hands, sitting or standing near one another - whereas American children", he adds, "establish a distinctly greater social distance."

Even Danes seem comfortable with an intimate zone of as little as 20-30 centimeters. By comparison the Norwegians, widely regarded as a more cautious society (and not just by the Danes), are very jealous of their bubbles of space - to an extent that astonished an American visitor. "One of the first things I noticed when I moved to Norway was that Norwegians need a lot of personal space", he remarked to an interviewer[8]. "Once I went into someone's office for an informal chat and sat down on the edge of his desk, some two meters from him. As I did that, I thought he would try to crawl out the window behind him! I had the distinct impression that I was on his territory. Also, I have found that if one reaches out to touch another during conversation, there will almost immediately be a recoil from the listener." Maybe that's why Norwegians, whenever they get the chance, prefer life in the Great and Underpopulated Outdoors.

"Of the four post-industrial factors of 'European production', *pragmatism* is strongly rooted in English culture but has a clear affinity with the Dutch and the Scandinavians. Such empiricism has given rise to the experiential manager. While its positive manifestation is in free-spirited individualism its negative form of expression is in rampant materialism.

Rationalism is strongly grounded in Gallic soil, and also in parts of Germany, Scandinavia, Northern Italy and also the French-speaking part of Switzerland. It has given rise, in its turn, to the professional manager. While its positive manifestation is that of a meritocracy its negative expression is in its stereotypical bureaucracy.

Wholism has emerged from a longstanding Germanic philosophical tradition, inclusive of Austro-Hungary and part of Switzerland. It has given rise to what may be termed a developmental manager. While its positive manifestation is wholistic, its negative expression is totalitarianism.

Finally, *humanism* is strongly rooted in Italian art and culture, whence came the first European Renaissance, while having distinct branches in Greece, Spain and Ireland. It has given rise to what may be called the convivial manager. While its positive manifestation is in its communal nature, its negative expression is in the form of nepotism and corruption."

Ronnie Lessem and Fred Neubauer. *European Management Systems*. Maidenhead: McGraw-Hill, 1993.

Chapter 3

The Field Work

Having made a brief overview of the most relevant research work, let's roll up our sleeves and wade into the muddy waters of the European business scene. Here I am drawing on the observations of many widely travelled and well informed members of the business and professional communities to supplement - or challenge - the conclusions I arrived at in my earlier book.

Before and during the course of preparing these two books, I have talked to hundreds of people, men and women, active in international organisations, commercial and other. My choice of informants has not been haphazard. I have tried to avoid relying excessively on that segment of the international community that spends its days commuting around a virtuous circle of 'club class' plane seats, three- (or even five-) star hotels and corporate conference rooms.

I have elected to draw on the experience of executives at the sharp end of the commercial world: marketing and sales people, negotiators, also engineers in multinational organisations and, as important vectors, those active in human resources management. I have also interviewed leading executive searchers, management consultants and research executives.

I have had more contact with the non-consumer end of business because, from my personal experience, this offers greater confrontation with cultural differences than one can gain from exposure to advertising agencies and the 'ad-mass'.

I have also intensified my contacts with people who, by their origins, are more open to an international environment and therefore more sensitive to cultural differences, in particular people from the smaller and less ethnocentric areas of Europe: Nordics, the people of the Benelux countries and, perhaps surprisingly, quite a number of American citizens: from many years' experience, I know as well as anyone else that Americans who have 'gone native' can be more European than the Europeans themselves.

This study also draws on the work of many other writers and specialists active in the cultural field, to whom I am indebted and who have, I hope, been properly interpreted and credited in every case.

27

It has to be said, in defence of all of us, that the statements that follow should be treated with the caution they deserve. These are broad strokes of the brush. Moreover, most European countries harbour more than one culture. The way Bavarians do business is dramatically different from that of Berliners, while the emergence of a distinctive SME culture in Swabia has much to do with family inheritance systems in the region.

Speaking of the Michelin organisation in their book *Management in France*[9], Jean-Louis Barsoux and Peter Lawrence point out that "the region of Auvergne is believed to exercise a profound influence on corporate values. Certainly the company mirrors the cautious, thrifty, sober and conservative attitudes that characterize the region." There is also a world of difference between Paris and Provence.

Talking about related phenomena in his book *The French*[10], Theodore Zeldin says: "Sociologists have... 'identified' five different forms of municipal government: 'hereditary monarchy' in the Vendée, the 'elective' type in Lorraine, 'egalitarian democracy' in the Jura, 'oligarchy on the Mediterranean coast' [remember Jacques Medecin?], and 'federalism' in the Limousin."

So cultures, even business cultures, reflect their immediate environment. So do observers, like myself and the people I have interviewed while preparing this book. As the Americans say, 'where you stand depends on where you sit'. By the same token, what you see depends on where you stand. We all inevitably have our own point of view.

Finally as Samuel Butler, the 19th century British writer, said, "a definition is the enclosing of a wilderness of an idea within a wall of words". But nothing ventured, nothing gained...

"We're stuck mentally in the industrial age... If we don't escape that mentality, then indeed I will have played the part of the Cassandra who foresaw the calamity"
Konrad Seitz

"The Germans have a much closer affinity to industry than the British or the French. This helps to explain why the most talented people go into manufacturing, not politics"
David Marsh, *The Germans*

"German managers are specialists. When they achieve general management responsibility, they need extra training as generalists"
Dutch management consultant

"They are perfectionist almost to the point of neurosis, but this does carry advantages"
John Ardagh, *Germany and the Germans*

*"German managers don't manage - they manage **something**"*
French management trainer

"They have perfected a system of economic and political consensus which - partly because of worries about the consequences if society ever became less organised - has become notoriously inflexible"
David Marsh, *The Germans*

"In Germany, when someone gets it wrong, nothing happens! You have to bang most Germans on the head to get them to accept the idea of doing things differently from what they're used to"
Belgian marketing director

"We need drastic changes in the way the dinosaur is run, and we need them fast"
Management board member of major German corporation

"Few Germans would sell their umbrella in the desert - it just might rain"
Philip Glouchevitch, *Juggernaut*

"Our firm has been functionally organised for the past 95 years"
Answer to industrial survey

GERMANY

It seems appropriate to start an examination of European cultural mindsets with the Germans: they have after all matured, through sheer hard work and strength of character, into Europe's industrial powerhouse, generating sufficient riches to become the Continent's wealthiest society and, at the same time, bail out much of the rest of Europe, east and west. Typically the rest of Europe, particularly the west, has difficulty in acknowledging this debt...

At the time of writing, the case for Germany looks weaker in the context of a changing world environment, and less coherent because of the evident conflicts of attitude between Ossies and Wessies. It is still, in my opinion, the best starting point for an examination of European social and business attitudes generally.

In Hofstede's book, the Germans rate as relatively high on the uncertainty avoidance scale, with a figure of 65 compared with, at the top end, Greece with 112 and, at the low end, Denmark with 23. They also, perhaps surprisingly for such a socially conscious country, rate relatively high on masculinity: 66, compared with a 'high' of 79 for Austria and a 'low' of 5 for Sweden.

The uncertainty avoidance score makes sense. Germany, as I pointed out in the previous chapter, is a highly codified society. It is also one which is renowned for the phenomenon of *Angst*, a word that is not easily translated ('anguish' doesn't quite do it, though the French do pretty well with the word *angoisse*). John Ardagh, the British journalist[11], quotes a German student he met who admitted that "what gives me Angst is worrying about whether or not I ought to feel Angst." While not endemic, this sense of unease is always lurking there in the shadows of German society.

No doubt Angst contributed to the excessive structuring of the German environment... and this same structuring predisposes people to Angst when the situation becomes mildly unmanageable. The combination has produced an essentially legalistic approach not only to matters of business but also to the whole business of living. This orientation is reflected in one remarkable statistic quoted by Hofstede: 65 per cent of senior German civil servants are law graduates, compared with a figure of three per cent for the UK.

This mindset has, moreover, led to two phenomena which mark German business life. First, a devotion to order, which in practice expresses itself in working methods that tend to be of an overstructured and sequential nature (and can encourage a stifling degree of bureaucracy, as experienced in such major corporations as Siemens). Secondly, a degree of unanimity amongst fellow-Germans which penetrates the fabric of everyday life and which I call the 'Social Consensus Effect' (SCE).

The advantage of SCE is that it encourages social order and correctness. Lenin is reputed to have said that the Germans always buy platform tickets before they storm a railway station. Whether he was right or not, an everyday reality of daily life is such aberrations (from the standpoint of an Anglo-Saxon) as rules that forbid mowing a lawn on Sundays or between the hours of 1 and 3 pm, putting glass in a dustbin after 8 pm, taking a shower in your own flat after 10 pm and, in the case of the good city of Hamm, allowing your dog to bark between 7 pm and 8 am.

The same value system shows through the comments of a Bayer executive interviewed by Samuel Humes for his book *Managing the Multinational*[12]: "We Germans respect disciplined professional expertise, capable of setting and achieving demanding objectives. Many non-Germans, especially Americans, have difficulty setting about a task without their objectives being determined for them. Germans prefer to set their own."

The drive to perfectionism is so firmly instilled in the German psyche that it tends to inhibit the development of the persona, both socially and professionally: one of the issues confronting German business schools is the need to foster a sense of creativity which, by definition, means departing from established procedures.

Peer pressure of course also has its advantages. When the direction (in both senses of the word) is both clear and determined, Germans have a facility for moving in impressive unison. Few musical experiences could compare with a performance of the Berliner Philharmoniker under the direction of Herbert Von Karajan. Even in less emphatically directed situations, Germans bring together a momentum and a rhythm which is dramatically impressive.

The downside to this momentum is of course the fact that, when the economic or psychological environment changes as it has a habit of doing from time to time, German businesspeople are often less spontaneous in adjusting to new conditions. This has been dramatically demonstrated on a number of occasions over the years: once with the camera industry (which stuck to traditional German electromechanical ways), twice with Volkswagen and even with a star like Daimler-Benz. Significantly each of these companies, having got its house in order, has shown that it once again qualifies as a worldbeater in these radically changed times.

A Belgian international marketing director throws light on the intricate personal mechanisms involved: "The Germans generally want the best of everything but, in today's unstable business environment, they're no longer sure what they want. They're disoriented by change. When the situation is not 'in the book', or is not what they're used to, they don't know what to do. And when a German manager is told by his director to cut his budget by 25 per cent, he feels challenged: what did I do, how does this make me look, what did I do wrong?"

As *The Economist* said, even before the Metallgesellschaft debacle in early-1994: "The lesson from both MG and Daimler-Benz is that the famous German virtues of long-term planning and research can be a weakness, too." But there's more to it than that, namely a reluctance to face up to change. With the help of what I call the SCE, people are motivated not to rock the boat: if they do draw attention to the hard facts, they get no thanks for their trouble. A German VP with a major US multinational sums it up: "People don't question their manager, they just do it!"

The combined catalysts of uncertainty avoidance, *Angst* and peer pressure have produced over time a society that is both symbiotic and hermetic: symbiotic through the intricate interweaving of the various estates, particularly big business and the banks, and hermetic in its resistance to intrusion from outside.

This hermeticism is the strength of German business and its weakness. So much was achieved simply because industry believed its products were better and rarely entertained the idea that foreigners might have something superior to offer.

I know the case of a foreign supplier who negotiated for months with one of Germany's leading automobile manufacturers. The latter's engineers found that the supplier's components passed all the quality and performance tests, the buyers were entirely happy with the price, but the company's board gave the thumbs down on acceptance of the supplier as a *third* source. Even allowing for the fact that all automobile companies are cautious about new sources of supply and, perhaps more importantly, that the supplier was British at a time when the country still had a poor labour record, the action of the German board in overriding its own technicians and buyers must say something.

This kind of mistrustful mentality was all well and good, as long as German industry was able to keep the initiative, but a dangerous mindset in today's conditions. The Finnish managing director of a US multinational comments that, confronted with increasingly intense competition from comparable products, German companies now respond by simply cutting their margins.

Many companies - British, French and others - have tried in the past to outmanoeuvre the German system to their cost. The Frankfurt correspondent of the *Financial Times* reported that, every time he tried to speak to a German bank other than the Deutsche Bank, the Dresdner Bank or the Commerzbank, he was referred back to... the Deutsche Bank, the Dresdner Bank or the Commerzbank. By collectively 'playing the game', the German business community ensures its own strength. It is a surprise for many foreigners to note the tradition of frank interchange of information between seeming competitors. *E pluribus unum*, it makes sense. Yet openness is an infrequent characteristic of German business, where corporations regularly conceal their profits for a rainy day...

One other important German trait - the reverse of the coin (the side which is rarely evoked by the stereotypes) and a natural antidote to so much order - is a philosophical, idealistic, sometimes even mystic predisposition. This is evident in peoples' attitudes to their bodies, to medicine and to the places they choose to go to on holiday, as well as in their civism and their commitment to society.

Working with the Germans

• Never start a business relationship by addressing your opposite number by his or her first name - that would be the end of the affair. Wait for him or her to invite you to do so, probably a matter of months or even years. Then feel flattered!

• On no account be patronising. Germans consider themselves - and generally are - well motivated, disciplined and professional. And be cautious about suggesting what their objectives should be. They already have them and prefer to set their own.

• When making a proposition, be specific in your claims and expectations, and don't ask for too rapid a response. Germans like to think about things - and to refer to the appropriate specialist on their side. A French consultant sums it up: "The Germans don't 'manage', they manage *something*!"

• Don't ask total strangers to share their commercial secrets with you. Germans are remarkably open in their dealings with those they know, but not with those they don't.

Allied with the craving for order, this philosophical disposition helps explain the idealistic dimension of society, naturally attuned to cooperation, worker participation and such concepts as *Arbeitgeber* (work-givers) and *Arbeitnehmer* (work-takers), words for what everyone else calls employers and employees.

But being a practically minded people, the Germans rarely allow this inclination to interfere directly with the conduct of their professional lives, even if world competition is forcing them to think again about the way they run their economy. Whatever else, the Germans are a consequential people. As the American CEO of a software company said:

"They're so damned demanding, both on themselves and others, that we have reason to be grateful to them. They keep us on our toes!"

Emergence of the manager

Two characteristics mark German educational tradition: first the dominance of the engineering sciences in German manufacturing industry, second the only relatively recent emergence of the professional manager (which, come to think of it, may help explain the presence of so many Dutch managers in German companies, particularly those located in the northwest corner of the country). Let's deal with the second point first.

Despite the fact that industry has always been considered a perfectly suitable career for a promising and well connected young German, for reasons of status and recognition (as much as lack of educational opportunity) the concept of the professional manager, the salaried senior executive, only started to gain ground in the last 30 years or so. In his book *The Germans*[13], David Marsh points out that "...the Germans have a much closer affinity to industry than the British or the French. This helps to explain why the most talented people go into manufacturing, not politics."

German business and industry has been traditionally dominated by two groups, owner-managers (the rump of German industry, the *Mittelstand*, is still largely composed of family-owned firms) and the professional classes, particularly lawyers and bankers. Until recently, and even in some circles today outside the major corporations, the German salaried manager is looked upon as a slightly lower form of life - not unlike the status generally accorded, paradoxically, to the engineer in British industry.

In his book, John Ardagh quotes a comment from a Siemens human resources manager that leaves one in no doubt: "In the United States, management is a separate profession in itself. Here, it is not. In Germany, a manager will have the technical background of whatever his firm deals with: thus, in a bank, a manager will probably have studied economics at college; and here, at Siemens, engineering. Our sales manager is an engineer, our R&D manager a physicist; on our main board of eleven directors, only two are non-technical. This has many advantages, for it means that directors understand a firm's product."

This attitude was echoed in a *Financial Times* interview with Gertrud Höhler, one of Germany's few top women executives who, significantly, has since abandoned German business to become a board member of Britain's Grand Metropolitan group: "It is almost unheard of for someone with a liberal arts background [like Höhler] to make a business career in Germany, where a doctorate in engineering or business economics seems to be the sole passport to a management position."

Of course, everyone knows that Germany is the paradise of the specialist, whether in big business or in the SME sector, the *Mittelstand* (see below). This vision of life was no more marked than in the petrochemical giants where divisional structuring contributed to a narrowly focused and excessively vertical progression up the hierarchical ladder - a phenomenon which Germans themselves recognise as a *Kaminkarriere* ('chimney career')! But the same applies in varying degrees to non-manufacturing functions, to the extent that one of the main concerns of corporate management and the business schools is to encourage people to break out of the mental confines of their speciality, whether it is finance, product development or whatever.

Germany in particular extols the engineer: even today a doctorate in engineering is the *nec plus ultra*. "The German solution to improving a company", says Philip Glouchevitch in his book *Juggernaut*[14], "is to build a better product."

I am reminded of a story, possibly apocryphal, about the different responses of a British board of directors and a German management board to the same situation: the news of the launch of a major product by a competitive company. The British directors, so the story goes, pondered awhile until somebody said "let's buy the company", to which proposal everybody said "hear hear". The German board went into a state of deep depression until, three weeks later, the engineering director came back with the first production model of an even better product. The British got **round** the problem, the Germans went straight to **the heart** of the problem.

The engineering tradition ensures that the Germans have a very systematic, even modular, approach to just about everything, including the use of the *Baukasten* (building block) principle in the construction, engineering and other industries. To some extent the modular approach reflects the technological past - another example of innate German conservatism.

There is a strong attachment, in many areas of industry and science, to things electro-mechanical, a technology in which the Germans have excelled. Under the communists even the East German computer industry made good **printers**, if nothing else. And German scientists and doctors still prefer things with buttons and knobs on them (they like to have some measure of control) than things that go buzz and whirr all on their own...

Training in the management sciences was restricted, until not long ago, to a doctor's degree in *Betriebswirtschaftlehre* at one of the German universities. Even today, the concept of the professional manager still has to win general acceptance. The human resources manager referred to in John Ardagh's book written in 1987 was quoted as saying: "We're quite happy with the present university system, and anyway we have no means of changing it. We do not need business schools."

In recent years, however, industry has recognised the need for specialised education and a number of well regarded business schools have emerged, in particular the USW Schloss Gracht at Erftstadt, outside Cologne, which was established at the initiative of a number of major German corporations in 1968. USW relates teaching as closely as possible to real-life conditions: computer-based simulation studies are used in addition to case studies and, as far as feasible, programmes reflect the professional environment participants come from. Particular emphasis is placed on developing entrepreneurialism, human skills and innovative thinking.

It is self-evident, however, that such initiatives by the captains of German industry have to be reflected in a change of mentality at the operational levels below. A German international journalist points another accusing finger at the human resources people in industry: "The CEOs may believe in opening up their companies to international thinking, but the personnel people still have their minds firmly closed. If you didn't study economics at a German university - and particularly if you studied abroad - you're regarded as an 'exotic'. They claim they want international experience, but they don't. "It is even rumoured that the Deutsche Bank has formalised such thinking to the point that their recruitment plans include a 5 per cent 'exotic quota' (*Exotenquote*)! That is what is called containment, German-style.

The manner in which Germans are taught, and expect to be taught, is also significant (see box, page 165). Hofstede recalls his experiences on an ITP (International Teachers Program) summer course for management teachers: "Most Germans... favor structured learning situations with precise objectives, detailed assignments, and strict timetables. They like situations in which there is one correct answer which they can find. They expect to be rewarded for accuracy. Their preferences are typical for strong uncertainty avoidance countries." He goes on to quote an only mildly ironic comment by a social psychologist, Wolfgang Stroebe[15] who said that "German students are brought up in the belief that anything which is easy enough for them to understand is dubious and probably unscientific."

At the same time the old *ex cathedra* style of education has largely been overtaken by a more socratic approach, where students are encouraged to exercise their minds rather than learn by rote (memorising is much more common to both

---

The American retailer, Toys'Я'Us, learned all about German hermeticism when it extended the relatively revolutionary concept of self-service in toys to Germany.

The trade used the argument that the absence of a *Fachmann*, a toy specialist, at the point of purchase could jeopardise a child's happiness and safety. International media comment at the time spoke of "powerful protectionist interests", "an array of uniquely German legal, technical and cultural barriers", "restrictive laws, government subsidies and rigid protocol of an old-boy network that dominates the economy." And this was a matter of child's play!

the French and American systems). But the typical German mind still combines intellectual intensity with sequential processing to a point that often eliminates feedback. Morever the importance placed by German society on degree status has produced generations of eternal students who stay on as long as necessary: in 1994, one in three undergraduates at the Free University of Berlin was over the age of 30.

A brief reference to the German apprenticeship system, the source of so much of the country's excellence (25 per cent of German CEOs have risen through the ranks), is *de rigueur* in a book like this. Applied across a vast range of activities, from office work to engineering, the system provides young people with vocational training from the age of 15 upwards. It combines in-company learning and operational practice, under supervision, with regular visits to a state school. It is an intensive, sustained approach to the development of skills which is uniquely German and as effective today as it was when it began to take shape much earlier in the country's history. Individual companies invest in the future of their youngest employees - and these employees know that, as likely as not, they will have a job for life. Another reason, along with their gift for 'hidden protectionism' and for industrial and social consensus, to think of the Germans as the Japanese of Europe.

United we stand

The macro-organisation of the German business world is the aspect that strikes foreigners most emphatically, particularly the symbiotic relationship between big business and the banks.

In a feature in mid-1993 hinting at changes ahead, *The Economist* commented: "German capitalism is built on debt, not equity. It is held together by close ties between companies and their banks. A mere 425 German companies have publicly listed shares, compared with 1,950 in Britain's smaller economy. And many of these are shielded from shareholders by friendly banks and insurers that own big stakes and, through proxy rights, control even bigger ones."

It is a relationship that has served the country extremely well since WWII but is now showing the strain, a relationship which contains the seeds of both ingroup complacency and conflict of interest, as borne out by the saga of Metallgesellschaft AG, news of which surfaced rather belatedly in the early weeks of 1994.

As *Wirtschaftswoche* said at the time, commenting on the solidarity typical of the country's big business community: "When Germany's supervisory boards fail, then they do so unanimously!" In fact, what seems to be failing is the two-tier supervisory/executive board system which, as events at Metallgesellschaft, Volkswagen and others have shown, creates a dichotomy at the top which only skilled communications - not a natural German strength - can overcome.

The *International Herald Tribune* summed up the implications of the symbiotic relationship between banks and business in the following words: "The bankers who hand out corporate credits, control shareholder voting rights, lead issuing consortia and are major company shareholders are the same officials who sit on the companies' supervisory boards." There have been suggestions that the maximum number of board seats occupied by one individual - set at ten to avoid abuse - should now be reduced to five.

At the time of writing, the future of Germany's machine-tool industry is in the hand of the banks. Having encouraged manufacturers to invest - in 1991 a unit of the Deutsche Bank forecast a 50 per cent increase in world demand for industrial machinery by the year 2000 and many companies geared up accordingly - the German banks are still having to help these same companies service their debt.

Egged on by its bankers, and anxious to maintain the *status quo*, German big business is careful to minimise its exposure to risk from outside - independently minded shareholders as much as foreign competitors. Philip Glouchevitch examines the infrastructure of German industry in detail: "German companies seem to be forever buying stakes in other companies instead of investing in their own businesses. Not all the stakes are visible, since stakes below 20 percent need not be reported... In collectively grabbing on to one another, German corporations are also in a sense over-coming their basic fear of the unknown." Weak uncertainty avoidance.

One of the consequences is that Germany's stock market only plays a limited role in the country's economic life, despite Frankfurt's new dynamism. The *Financial Times* states that, of the 664 German companies which are stock market listed (compared with 3,000 in the UK), many are majority owned by families, by other companies or by financial institutions «with the result that the management priorities of quoted companies tend to be lttle different from those of private ones."

Further on in his book, Glouchevitch talks about corporate reticence on the issue of profits: "German business is structured to encourage capital formation in such a way that companies amass - at least when business is good - vast reserves of hidden assets. When business is bad, the companies can discreetly fall back on hidden reserves, and no one is the wiser." He then goes on to quote a financial specialist who describes the German accounting system as a polite little lie between companies on the one hand and the government and labour unions on the other.

As in the case of Daimler-Benz, moving out of this cosy environment to face the stringent reporting rules of Wall Street can be a trauma for the company and a revelation for outsiders. In fact, the tolerant nature of German law on matters of transparency is in strict contrast to the tendency to regulate and codify everything else. The common factor is the desire to eliminate the unexpected and favour the establishment - not an ideal environment for innovation!

The ultimate result of all this is that the fortunes of German industry are indeed invested in a select group of individuals - members of the supervisory boards together with the growing cadre of professional managers prominent in the larger companies and, through cross-holdings, influential in the affairs of many others.

This cadre has indeed grown too big in some of the major corporations, with unhealthily discrete 'vertical' product divisions and indiscriminate layering of upper and middle management levels, leading to excessive bureaucracy, poor communications and, ultimately, inefficiency. One of the first companies to see the light is Bayer, which has already reduced its product groups from 23 to 20, its top management grades from six to four, and is stripping a number of organisational layers, with the aim of cutting upper and middle management numbers by ten per cent in the medium term.

Similar draconian action is needed in many other major German corporations but, with an innate resistance to change and the status accorded to rank and title in German big business, this will not be easy to achieve. Another traditional feature of these big corporations is the clear operational distinction made between domestic sales (*VI*) and exports (*VE*), not unlike the lingering mentality of British business. In the context of the Single Market, this kind of thinking is redundant.

A fitting conclusion is provided by the observation made by Ekkehard Wenger, professor of banking and corporate studies at the University of Würzburg, to *The European* newspaper: "You might say most German corporations are run with the rigid management structures known from pre-war times. They are run like dynasties and, like dynasties, management is often inflexible."

No chapter on German industry would be complete without reference to the *Mittelstand*, a word implying the rump of small-to-medium companies, but which refers to a phenomenon that has been defined by business academics in at least 200 different ways, the common factor being the management approach, with a commitment to independence and technological excellence, rather than size. Indeed quite a number of these German SMEs exceed the 500-employee ceiling and would be classed as big business anywhere else. They are responsible for at least half the country's industrial production, employ two-thirds of the workforce and account for over two-thirds of exports.

It is in this sector of German industry that regional differences show up most. As in private life, the business style of a Bavarian is as different from that of a Rhinelander as that of a Rhinelander is from that of a Berliner.

However these German SME companies generally have one thing in common, which is private - generally family -

ownership. They also are extremely secretive (like most European SMEs, they have an innate fear of officialdom and, in particular, the tax inspector) and they are by nature conservative. Anxious to secure the family fortune and heritage, they specialise intensely, stick to accepted routines and rarely take risks. Yet they, more than any other sector of the German economy, responded to the call to bail out the bankrupt industries of eastern Germany...

Indeed their innate conservatism does not even prevent German SMEs from treating the world's markets as their oyster, once they have won a reputation in their chosen field, and even investing money in manufacturing facilities outside Germany (again, sometimes as a way of bypassing the tax inspector). In a country which spurned professional managers for far too long, the German SME owner-manager is generally regarded with due respect by the establishment: the banks and the authorities.

As in the case of the big business/banks symbiosis, this cosy arrangement is likely to change. Profit margins are shrinking and many founder-managers are nearing the end of their active lives. The new generations - and time - will tell!

German bosses more loyal than French, survey finds

Top German corporate bosses are more loyal to their firms, closer to their workers and more highly motivated than their French counterparts, according to a survey published this week.

[Executive search consultants] Heidrick & Struggles surveyed the managing directors of the top 200 companies in each country and found that bosses in Germany were much more likely to have been groomed by their current firm than those in France.

More than 70% of bosses in Germany began their careers at the level of middle management or lower in the firm they now lead, compared with just 30% in France.

Some 36% of French managing directors were 'parachuted' into their posts from outside the firm, while only 16% of German chief executives got their jobs that way. The number of managing directors poached from state jobs was six times higher in France than in Germany.

The report said Germany stressed training in industry, whereas highfliers in France typically graduate from elite schools into top state jobs before moving to industry.

Managers' status differed sharply between the two countries. "The hierarchical distance between the shop floor and board room in a French company is much greater than in Germany," the study said. "The top man in the French model... knows infinitely more about the upper reaches of government and the way it functions than about the shop floor."

Wall Street Journal Europe, 18 January 1992

The Heidrick & Struggles study referred to on the preceding page also showed that, even today, three *Grandes Ecoles* - the Polytechnique, the ENA and the HEC - still produce between them more than half of all the chief executives of France's "Top 200" companies.

The Polytechnicien - also known as the 'X' - is the *crème de la crème*. He knows, even today in the 1990s, that he rules by divine right. The words of a business luminary Auguste Detoeuf, quoted by David Granick back in the 1960s, still convey something of the spiritual, cartesian and irrational flavour of the French establishment: "To begin with, the X knows nothing and he knows that he knows nothing. Knowing nothing (on the express condition of knowing that one knows nothing) is a marvellous means of command. The man with knowledge loses himself in the details of his science; one of the great difficulties for someone who rises in grade is that he must forget that he knows the craft of his subordinate and must renounce exercising it."

● ● ● ●

"In essence, the French, although more sensitive to people, are slightly more into power/political styles of management, but less disciplined than the Germans who freely admit less sensitivity to people but a greater adherence to organisational discipline and systems."

Only 26% of German top managers are recognised as being sensitive to people, compared with 41% of French top managers.

*Professor Andrew Kakabadse,
Cranfield School of Management*[16]

"The design of a French organisation resembles the country's constitution in that it confers power upon a single person"

French lawyer

"French managers can solve any problem - assuming they can detect the problem in the first place"

Anonymous

"Often the French seem to concentrate on phenomena rather than causes and solutions. Perhaps this is due to their education. They learn to analyse and to express themselves verbally very brilliantly and have a need to do so"

German businessman

"It's strange. Their society preaches equality, yet individually they can be very autocratic"

Belgian multinational manager

"We French have the best engineers. The trouble is that we don't have much commercial sense"

French export trade official

"The French admire the Germans for their competence but, at the same time, criticise them both for their pushiness and for their unrelenting openness in business matters"

German woman executive

"French bosses have not caught up with the elementary notion that the customer is king"

The Economist

"In France, it's much more than chauvinism. There's a negative attitude toward anything that's not French"

Belgian entrepreneur

"The French do not always respect the evidence. Once they get something into their heads, that's it!"

Professor Geert Hofstede

"To be or not to be, that is the question. But the question is badly formulated"

If Shakespeare had been a Frenchman...

FRANCE

At least it can be said that the German mind is essentially, even relentlessly, consistent. In that respect it differs from most other European cultures, which harbour a contradiction that creates an inner tension within the national psyche - what I call 'psycho-poles'.

In the case of the French, this contradiction resides in their intellectual commitment to equality and social consensus on the one hand, and a visceral urge to assert their individuality on the other.

"The French tend to believe that the basic truths on which life is based derive from principles and immutable or universal laws", is the comment of intercultural management consultants Philip Harris and Robert Moran. "They profess lofty ideals of fraternity and equality, but at times show characteristics of utmost individualism and selfish materialism."

So, confronted with what looks at first sight like the most elitist, autocratic and aloof society in Europe, foreigners are baffled and perplexed. Does the lip-service to egalitarianism have any meaning or is it all humbug?

It seems that, through some quirk of their culture, the French are quite comfortable accommodating this contradiction. Indeed it has been formally factored into everyday life. As sociologist Michel Crozier remarks[17]: "At all levels of society the French, once they gain entry into an influential group, instinctively try to keep others out."

Hofstede found the French to be very high on both power distance **and** individualism at one and the same time. As Jean-Louis Barsoux and Peter Lawrence say in their impressive study of French business, *Management in France*: "Is it not intriguing that the French, who are less willing to take orders, are more willing to accept that some people have much more power than others?"

Hofstede also found the French were high on uncertainty avoidance. As Barsoux and Lawrence remark, "this finding is again intriguing, since a standard remedy for reducing uncertainty is to accept orders - but the French are reluctant to do this."

To understand these contradictions a little better, it helps to distinguish between the symbolic and the intimate French persona. The average educated French person - and there's no more ferociously educated a bunch than the French! - accommodates the two comfortably.

The process started as far back as the turn of this millenium, with the emergence of the Capetian dynasty and the creation of the embryonic kingdom of France. Since then, successive generations of French people, with encouragement from *le Roi Soleil* and Napoleon, have been indocrinated with the spirit of their Frenchness, their uniqueness, their intellectual prowess and *La Gloire*. To paraphrase the German author Ulrich Wickert, when the French speak of **La France,** they evoke a conceptual and symbolic complex, not just a place on the map.

So the symbolic overlaps and entwines with the intimate, to the point that many of those programmed in this way (and not always the most intelligent ones) cannot even themselves distinguish between the two. Occasionally it can have disastrous consequences; witness the saga of the Crédit Lyonnais bank under the stewardship of Jean-Yves Haberer, aided and abetted by various people in even higher places.

The foreign observer will do well to keep this propensity of the French firmly in mind and make the necessary allowances. This may sound condescending - when there is absolutely no reason to be condescending to the French (they don't need it) - but it can help one get to grips with the French mentality.

It is a simple fact that, in respect of certain dimensions of their collective subconscious, they **have** to be indulged. Being French is clearly a mindset in its own right. The complex is evident in the almost rabid official defence of the language, resulting in legislation that states that in any kind of business communication, "recourse to any foreign term or expression is prohibited so long as there is a French term or expression in the same sense."

This leads on to the second puzzling feature of the French persona in business, and one of which I suspect they are even less aware - namely their ability to allow their spirit of cartesianism to smother their innate commonsense. As an American businessman remarked to a reporter back in the mid-60s: "The Frenchman, by inclination and education, mistrusts simple things and tends to over-complicate." Here again, it is heritage that is largely to blame: the educated French lack absolutely nothing in intellect and intelligence.

The French taste for complicating things may of course partly reflect a peculiarly Gallic form of perfectionism: French design is often idiosyncratic and clever, but not always practical. But the predilection also suggests simple intellectual conceit, accompanied at times by a rather charming and childlike desire to show off.

The Economist, speaking of the French, talks of "a neurotic urge to be different". It even extends to a remarkable lack of tolerance for things as they are: a German academic complains bitterly of his French counterparts' tendency "to throw things away that are working perfectly well" (something the Germans rarely do, of course). "They seem to always want something new, I think because they themselves are anxious to look innovative..."

How the Germans see the French[*]

"The hierarchical thinking in French companies is uncompromisingly clear. The president has the final word and nobody should even question whether what the boss says is right or not. The French centralise the management of their companies. It is vital for the French manager that he is personally successful, the success of his company comes second..."

"... but French managers can be easily motivated, they make fast decisions which, however, they can change just as fast. Continuity is never guaranteed, even for foreign subsidiary strategies which are developed in France."

"The French would like to manage everything on their own, even their foreign subsidiaries. As this is impossible, they at least install a French comptroller whom the Germans often feel has a negative impact on the business."

[*] from *Capital*, the German business magazine.

This echoes the comment of British journalist and author John Ardagh[18]: "The French have a tendency to fall in love with new ideas and then not to bother too much with their application; in some firms, new American jargon and gadgetry barely conceal the persistance of old French habits of rigid hierarchy and routine."

A Franco-German consultancy team, Pierre De Bartha and Jochen Peter Breuer, make the point that, despite the strong uncertainty avoidance of the French, they tend to look for the opportunities in a business situation where the Germans are concerned by the risks. "Efficiency to the Germans is when a meeting, a project development or a working day goes exactly to plan... To the French, efficiency is when one achieves more than might have been expected [even if, as is likely, no clearly measurable objectives in the German sense had been set]. They then congratulate themselves in words like 'fantastic, look how flexibly and intelligently we solved that one'."

This is in stark contrast to the French attitude toward planning in the grand or strategic sense, where the plan assumes more importance than the results. Hofstede's epic research measured, among many other things, "the desire to control the future by a miscellany of planning, procedures and contingency arrangements." Here the French with their high uncertainty avoidance scored 86 on the scale, compared with the Germans at 65 and the weak uncertainty avoidance British at 35.

Changing one's mind is not viewed by the French as unreliability, but as proof of intelligence and versatility. Indeed, most self-respecting French people are short on modesty, even disarmingly conceited about their intellectual prowess. I say 'disarmingly' because they are quite happy to admit it: an American publishing friend of mine had one of his employees concede, straightfaced, that "we French are full of ourselves, and justifiably so." Even though they may not actually boast about it, it still shows through, like it or not.

Much of this mindset is explained in a sentence written by a leading expert on French culture, Theodore Zeldin: "The French always place a school of thought, a formula, convention, *a priori* arguments, abstraction and artificiality above reality; they prefer clarity to truth, words to things, rhetoric to science."

It may not be insignificant that I know of two versions of the same *bon mot* revealing French self-awareness. The first, coined in the early postwar period, went: "in France we don't have energy, we have ideas." More recently (possibly triggered by jealousy at Britain's North Sea oil finds), the phrase has resurfaced as "in France we don't have oil, we have ideas." The common factor is the French conviction that they have creative minds - in this case spawning Europe's most impressive nuclear power industry, with most of the stations discharging waste heat into the sea or the rivers flowing into their neighbours' backyards!

Like flies in amber

This, in some cases, is about all they know of their neighbours. As a nation the French, trapped in their culture like flies in a beautiful but eternal amber, display an amazing ignorance of what goes on around them. To the north they deform geography: I have met French graduates who have difficulty in placing The Netherlands on the map. To the south they deform the image of other cultures - to the detriment of the Italians and, particularly, the Spanish. What they think of Spain is illustrated by the reaction of a French businessman when told that a northern US business school planned to open a European branch in Spain: "But that's like going to Mexico!"

Linked with their rather childlike conceits is another feature of the French psyche that is less easy to digest: their occasional bloodymindedness. This should not be confused with lack of politeness - nothing should put you more on your guard than a Frenchman who is being excessively civil. As the world's doyens of diplomacy, the French know the art of charming the other party...

Essentially reasonable as individuals, the French can be breathtakingly obdurate and obtuse collectively, particularly in matters of national interest. Examples abound: Mitterand's skill in making a 15-minute speech at the end of the Gulf War with not a single reference to the American effort, Chirac's stonewalling on the European Central Bank to the discountenance of everybody else involved, the actions of public servants like the PTT buyer who told a British bidder firmly but with great charm: "We have no intention of according type approval to **your** machine until our national suppliers have perfected **their** machine. But, if you repeat this admission to anyone else, we will deny it categorically." Something of the same kind happened more recently over certification of a foreign AIDS test where, according to *Libération* newspaper, the authorities put commercial protection of a French-made product ahead of the needs of patients.

In the words of the *Wall Street Journal Europe*, "the French business establishment is still run by a powerful old-boy network that is hard to penetrate - and which can blackball would-be members who get too uppity." As Gianni Agnelli found out to his cost.

In their book *Management in France*, Jean-Louis Barsoux and Peter Lawrence highlight the impersonal nature of French business relations compared with both their own social behaviour and the Anglo-Saxon management tradition. "At its extreme French *cadres* [management executives] can exhibit astonishing awareness of their own 'split personality'."

They examine the notion of impersonality developed by Desmond Graves, who found that "the French tend to regard authority as residing in the role not the person."

This schizophrenically theoretical division is reflected in the comment of the former French health minister Georgina Dufoix that she was "responsible but not guilty" for the contaminated blood scandal that shook the country.

According to Graves, "it is by the power of his position that a French manager gets things done... This is in contrast to the Anglo-Saxon view that authority is vested in the person... The distinction between the two cultures implies that a Frenchman will accept responsibility so long as it is attached to his role but will not actively seek responsibility, as a British manager might, for it adds nothing to his stature."

Simple-minded foreigners, brought up in a different tradition, find this kind of behaviour not only bad-mannered, but decidedly cynical. It encourages the kind of reaction expressed by the Swedish lady shareholder at the time of the Volvo-Renault courtship: "I don't trust the French". It's not altogether surprising, particularly in someone coming from so different and genuinely egalitarian a culture.

Intellectual agility or spirituality, allied with a not entirely justified sense of cultural superiority, can indeed get the French into hot water: *insouciance* can easily lead to a state of hubris. A very successful Belgian executive with a multinational car hire company says that, when managing the firm's French subsidiary, he ran head on into the *laisser-aller* mentality of the French: "Because they think they are smart and *débrouillard*, they leave things like car bookings till the last minute and then wonder why there are no cars available!"

Linked with this is an ambivalent attitude towards serving others, particularly customers. Polly Platt, cross-cultural expert and close observer of the French scene, states matter-of-factly that "customer service is totally unknown in France".

"Disregard for the customer is a way of life in the French business world", asserted a French reader in a letter to the *International Herald Tribune* in April 1994. "While many say that services are the business of the future, France is headed for economic disaster unless the general attitude changes soon". Strong words!

Indeed, in French eyes, putting oneself readily at the disposal of a total stranger is an affront to one's self-esteem: like the Spanish (see below), the French have difficulty in recognising the difference between service and servility.

However indifference can evaporate fast in adversity. The American sales director of a US export corporation points out that "when things go against them and business gets tough, the French get increasingly nervous and defensive." The European CEO with the corporate HQ of a US multinational evokes a familiar theme: "They're good team people - particularly with their fellow nationals when they think their culture is under threat!" Realism and *la Gloire* cohabiting again...

How Americans see the French - and *vice versa*

"Whereas the American tries to think in a straight line, the Frenchman insists on thinking in a circle. The American mistrusts complex things and tends to over-simplify. The Frenchman, by inclination and education, mistrusts simple things and tends to over-complicate. It is for this reason that no Frenchman, by American standards, can ask a simple, straightforward question when speaking in public. By French standards, no American speaker can give a full, sophisticated answer. A Frenchman tries to define the question; the American tries to answer it.

A French businessman mistrusts the very things in which an American businessman has the most confidence. Examples? The Frenchman is innately suspicious of the figures on a balance sheet, of the telephone, of his subordinates, of the law, of journalists and of what he reads in the press, of investment banks, and, above all else, of what an American tells him in confidence. The American, *au contraire*, has trust in all these things.

An American executive tends to forget what he's said in a letter. A Frenchman never forgets what he's purposely left out. This particular law of communication explains why negotiations often break down at a distance. After a meeting in Paris the American will write a letter so factual and so detailed that, in his own mind at least, it doesn't even require an answer. The Frenchman would consider any letter he addressed to a company in the U.S. as the beginning of a long correspondence in which he would gradually elaborate on the nuance contained in the second line of paragraph three. The American will say about the French letter, 'It's very polite but what the heck is he trying to say?'. The Frenchman will ponder the American letter. 'There are many details, *mais qu'est-ce que ça veut dire*?' What's he trying to tell me?"

E. Russell Eggers, President, Loctite Corporation

Yet, when they manage to keep their nerve and their sense of proportion, the French are capable of taking on not only the rest of Europe but the rest of the world. Thanks to a unique blend of singlemindedness and creativity, they have outstripped everyone else in high-technology areas like digital telecommunications, space rocketry and high-speed trains. Much of this success they owe, of course, to their own particularly Gallic blend of social symbiosis, just as powerful as the German formula yet very different.

The cartesian spirit of the French encourages them in the belief that, because they have thought things out so thoroughly, their opinion must be right. Allied to a still vigorous attachment to the traditions of centralising Jacobinism, inherited from revolutionary times, this results in a predisposition to dirigism.

This spirit of dirigism, harnessing the industrial and scientific talent of the country, explains both the great achievements and the great fiascos of recent French history. I have already mentioned some of the achievements. Fiascos, I suggest, include the attempt to conquer the world with SECAM TV technology, the Bull computer saga, and a number of wishful cross-frontier alliances. Renault lost the Skoda automobile deal because they went to the top instead of working at the base.

As Marian Caffe, the Czech prime minister, undiplomatically pointed out: "First, the French came late. Second, the French began by visiting the ministries; the Germans (began) with the company. Third, the French came here; the Germans invited our people to go to Germany." This uniquely Gallic mixture of dirigism with aloofness may work inside France, but not necessarily outside.

Les grandes écoles

Such techniques work well enough within France precisely because of the closely knit nature of the country's elite society, bringing together government and business in a relationship that is as symbiotic as that within the German establishment, yet very different. It is based as much on awareness of privilege as it is on self-interest.

61

The key to this remarkable degree of symbiosis is to be found in that uniquely French institution, the *grandes écoles* - and in particular the ENA, the HEC and the Polytechnique, the *nec plus ultra* for a prestigious education in engineering. These far surpass in both distinctiveness and influence any social infrastructure invented by any other European nation, including the British 'public school' system. They provide an apprenticeship for a distinguished career in government and big business, creating and perpetuating an administrative elite which effectively holds the reins of the country in its hands.

Graduates of these *grandes écoles* often start their careers in one of the ministries. The case of the young man who earns his laurels as an *Inspecteur des Finances*, policing the tax irregularities of big business, only later to go onto the board of the selfsame company by a process that is known as *parachutage* or *pantouflage*, sounds like fiction to a foreigner. Yet it is the stuff of the establishment *à la française*. It obviously satisfies the low uncertainty avoidance tastes of the French: a career path is there for life (see box page 48).

While a majority of French managers have an education in the natural sciences, a lot of the academic emphasis is on mathematics which, in the words of a French lawyer, "are deemed a faithful indicator of the ability to synthesise ideas and to engage in abstract reasoning, a valued skill in France." Whatever else their shortcomings, the French are sublimely numerate. The tradition originated with the engineer, both military and civil, then extended into other fields of endeavour.

In fact, the military influence is very evident in many aspects of French education. The same lawyer remarks that "from education to taxation, France is permeated by state control and military values... the most brilliant minds are the products of a military environment - be they in the government or in business." He must be thinking particularly of the 'X', the students of the Polytechnique, who parade in uniform at their graduation ceremony.

As a creation of the French establishment, with rigorous entry standards, the *grandes écoles* dominate French establishment life in a spirit of auto-defence. The universities, born of a longstanding and more liberal tradition, definitely take back seat in the formation of the country's future. Relatively laxist and loosely organised, they are open to anyone passing his *baccalauréat*, the final secondary school exam. They still however perpetuate the *ex cathedra* style of education, creating a massive memorisation challenge for students.

The government, which does not seem unduly concerned by this state of affairs, also channels most of its research funds into a series of state-controlled research institutes, rather than onto university campuses. The problem is compounded by the fact that, in the words of François Kourilsky, director-general of the CNRS research agency, "the research concentration in Paris makes it difficult for universities in other regions to provide a full offering of courses in every field."

As Barsoux and Lawrence remark, the *grandes écoles* "have been so convincing in promoting themselves as 'surrogate management schools' that one can understand in part

---

"A long-standing feature of French society is the high premium it places on intellect. Where America extols money, West Germany work and Great Britain blood, France has nailed its flag to the post of cleverness."

"For the Americans, universality resides in the training. Conventional wisdom in the United States is that management is a discipline that can be taught and learned and has principles which are generally applicable. For the French, on the other hand, it is the man who, by virtue of his intellectual quality, can adapt to any situation. Polyvalence stems from the person as an 'intellectually finished product', not the imparting of particular skills and techniques. In some ways, the French manager is closer to a professional version of the British tradition of the 'gifted all-rounder' who can turn his hand to anything - but in France the *raison d'être* is measured intellectual performance, and in Britain a diffuse notion of leadership."

Jean-Louis Barsoux and Peter Lawrence, *Management in France*.

---

the belated emergence of American-style business schools in France." It is all the more encouraging then that France has recently fostered some of the most impressive new management educational ventures. ESC Lyon, ESC Nantes, ISA and ISG Paris, and the EAP and AMSEC groups of schools have now joined CPA Paris, the first postgraduate school of business administration to be established in Europe, and that venerable international institution INSEAD. Unfortunately the list is now much longer with the number of institutions climbing onto the bandwaggon...

Chiefs and Indians

The autocratic instincts of the average French *Président-Directeur-Général* (PDG) and the power distance accepted by his or her employees marks French industry from the biggest corporations to the smallest SMEs. As Barsoux and Lawrence explain, "the PDG is what Britons would regard as 'chairman of the board' and 'managing director' rolled into one."

Perceived discretionary control down to the minutest detail is the name of the game. In his book *Mind your Manners*[19], John Mole refers to a survey of European managers *, in which "one of the questions was: 'Is it important for a manager to have at his fingertips precise answers to most of the questions that subordinates raise about their work'. Of Frenchmen, 60 per cent said it was, the highest percentage along with Italians. A French PDG shows much more attention to detail than equivalents in other countries."

The practical implications of this concentration of power are illustrated by Frenchman Dominique Frischer in his book *La France vue d'en Face*[20]: "The weight of company hierarchy is such that a word from a top manager can annul projects which have been discussed and developed for hours by senior management, whose opinion is worth nothing against the omnipotence of the ENA graduate at the top of the pyramid."

With this degree of power distance, the natural concomitant to hierarchy is formality. In fact, when compared with life in most other European countries, French society seems

* undertaken by André Laurent.

obsessively formal at its upper levels - although an American CEO pointed out to me that strangers actually talk to one another in the train these days.

The complexity of relationships within many French corporations makes it difficult for foreigners to know how to proceed. The German vice president of a major US multinational comments that "there are often too many people involved and it's not clear who makes the decisions." As a first step, it is important to be able to make the distinction between a *décideur* and an *exécutant* (it's rather like the difference between an Anglo-Saxon management consultant and his client!).

This is confirmed by a French lawyer, who offers a couple of tips which are typically, trenchantly French : "First, don't ask a senior manager to make an operational decision because that's not his job! Second, don't **deal** with a French executive: take him out to dinner and talk to him about everything except business. Even if you are a senior executive, your opposite number in a French company will be lower down in the management structure. Deal with **him**!"

A British marketing consultant explains this dilemma in the following terms: "French subordinates are always saying: 'I have to ask the boss', though they will try to beat the system if they can. They only refer upstairs when they're afraid of being found out!"

An American executive with a French publishing house says that "the French employee, conditioned by a lifetime of distance from his superiors, will hang back, believing that the less known about himself, the longer he can safely hide in his protective cocoon." He then adds, "consistent with the air of mistrust is the French employee's aversion to responsibility [here comes Hofstede's uncertainty avoidance again]. He knows that upward movement in the company will constrain his much-prized individuality... he will refuse to cross the boundaries into the realm of initiative." Many people comment on the reluctance of French middle managers to commit themselves.

Even the products of the *grandes écoles* share this instinct of self-preservation. In the words of Barsoux and Lawrence,

Underground and underprepared

One of the odd things about the Channel Tunnel is that, rather than bringing Europeans closer together, it seems to be setting them further apart. It started before even the first sod was turned: "The French spent money and planned before they began", said a Eurotunnel executive at the time. "The British just walked on to the site and started up."

As French management expert Jean-Louis Barsoux has said in another context, "the French like to be able to see the end of the tunnel before they enter it."

The strip of water that separates the two countries (*La Manche* to the French) is known, in English, as the 'English' and not the 'British' Channel. That lets the Scots, the Welsh and the people of Northern Ireland off the hook.

The cult of walking on site underprepared - apart from a knack for responding pragmatically to circumstances - is a peculiarly English phenomenon. It may be seen as a stereotype, but it has some substance and is based on observation. Another stereotype, with substance and prejudice, is evident in the words of a member of the British drilling team when the two met in the middle: "We've must have broken through. There's a whiff of garlic in the air."

Throughout the development of this high-speed rail link between the Anglo-Saxon and the Latin world, differences of attitude have been dramatic. While the British procrastinated and examined their consciences, the French went into action. Their realism, helped along by the usual dose of government dirigism, produced high-speed results. Local administrators fell over one another to make sure that the track ran through their constituency and not the one next door - in complete contrast to the gentry of 'the Garden of England', who did everything possible to ensure that the track went through somebody else's backgarden.

In fairness to the French, some of them still put quality of life first. The administrators of one *commune* on the proposed route did everything possible to frustrate the planners' intentions. With Gallic ingenuity, they bought a strategic plot of land and sold it in one-square-meter lots to people in places like Hawaai and Hong Kong, creating a legal web that not even the French government would have been able to unravel. Not content with this, the mayor gave instructions, in the event of his death, to have his remains buried on site. With all the excitement he had a heart attack and died. But French dirigism had the last word: the planners expropriated land alongside the plot and rerouted the line.

Even the styling and layout of the high-speed trains for the Eurotunnel link has stimulated cultural conflict. The *International Herald Tribune* reports how "the British favored a stylized replica of the classic Orient Express; the Belgians wanted the interior divided into traditional six-person compartments; the French wanted open airline-style seating. After months of discord, a gentleman's agreement was reached. The British would design the exterior, the Belgians would do the toilets and the baggage compartments and the French would handle the rest." As usual the British and the Belgians compromised - and the French won.

With the Tunnel now in the operational stage, these cultural differences are finally earning recognition. Nobody seems particularly concerned that, whereas the information displays at the French end of the Tunnel are uncompromisingly futuristic, the ones at the British end are unrepentently nostalgic. And as Eurotunnel's director of human resources, Yves-Noel Derenne, acknowledged in an interview, "for a team in the UK a uniform is important. In France, you belong to the team, but you don't want to be seen to belong."

Even the fact that a TGV fell into a foxhole on the outskirts of Lille didn't alarm the British for once - although some French people had grounds for momentary alarm when the train derailed at 300kph but stayed upright (another triumph of French technology). British visions of rabid foxes entering the UK via a Tunnel already well defended with anti-rabid-fox-fences were dispelled when it became known that the 'foxhole' was a WWI trench, and maybe even a British one at that.

"*grande école* graduates are generally not inclined to risk their talents in an entrepreneurial way to stimulate new business, but exploit them instead to gain authority in bureaucratic hierarchies."

When you hear things like this, you realise that Jacques Tati's parody in *Mon Oncle*, with cubicles for the underlings and long marble-tiled corridors noisely announcing the boss's approach, are not that far from the truth!

Perhaps because benevolent paternalism tends to take precedence over power distance in private business, France's SME sector is looked at slightly askance by the mandarins of the *grandes écoles*. Setting up one's own business is not the same thing as running a state enterprise and, on top of that, the historical record of France's SMEs is not that brilliant (brilliance being something that any self-respecting French person puts a premium on). Barsoux and Lawrence make the point that "it is ironical that the nation which spawned the word *entrepreneur* (Jean-Baptiste Say in 1800) should have been traditionally so weak in that domain."

So French SMEs - which tend to fall into one of two categories, often long-established medium-size bourgeois family businesses on the one hand and artisan-managed workshops on the other - still tend to suffer from a Cinderella reputation which is as much imposed as self-inflicted. Their status essentially reflects the structure of French business society and, in particular, the elitism of the people on the inside.

There are signs that, with the nuanced transfer of authority from Paris to the provinces, the status of French SMEs is being reassessed but, behind the mask of officialdom, these traditional attitudes are hard to change.

"What has really astounded me is the mixture of formality with a relaxed approach to doing business. They laugh more than Germans and board meetings are less structured, without the deadly seriousness which surrounds board meetings in Germany"

German woman executive with UK multinational

"I had five British guys in my office fighting about what they wanted. They excused themselves and went away to sort things out. The Germans work things out first"

Dutch managing director

"For all their simulated modesty, the British can be tough and blandly ruthless when necessary. They are masters at intelligence gathering, political blackmail, and chicanery..."

Philip Harris and Robert Moran

"The British attach more importance to a willingness to compromise than their counterparts from other countries"

British management academic

"The British character is too much against revolution, or even logical consistency, drastic steps, and uncompromising action"

Nikolaus Pevsner

"British executives can tolerate being proved wrong, unlike we hot-tempered Frenchmen"

Denis Brulet

"The English can never be convinced by arguments, only by facts"

Attributed to Jean Monnet

*"The Englishman when thinking, meditates on action .
The Frenchman, when acting, executes his thoughts"*

Salvador de Madariaga

"An Englishman's mind works best when it is almost too late"

Lord D'Abernon

*"Waive, Britannia
Britannia, waive the rules!"*

Anonymous

70

BRITAIN

As we have come to expect, the British present a total contrast to everything we have heard so far. Yet the British also harbour an internal contradiction, a set of 'psycho-poles' comparable to the equality/individualism equation of the French. In the case of the British, this is the divergence between their outward sense of fairness and compromise on the one hand, and unrestrained if occasional outbursts of naked ambition on the other (incidentally, it was a Spaniard and not a Frenchman who talked about 'perfidious Albion').

This dichotomy can be explained in part by what I call the Nostalgia Factor (NF), a deep-set fondness for things which shouldn't matter to a rational being, but evidently do. This erratic sentimentality and its accompanying symbolism emerge in many aspects of everyday life, both private and professional, the centre of attraction ranging from old trains through animals and royalty to the Old Boy's Club and the very concept of fairness itself.

Unfortunately as Beppe Severgnini, an Italian business journalist, noted in a piece in *The Economist*, "the trouble is that the British love of what is ancient and well-known turns into fear of what is new and unknown."

Lord Hailsham may have been too kind when he said that "the British are notable for their sentimentality, which they mistake for a virtue: hence their ability to deceive themselves, which others mistake for hypocrisy." There are unfortunately cases enough of outright hypocrisy, both in business and elsewhere. Its most evident manifestation is in politics, where British statesmen manage to be as two-faced as their French counterparts, without having the nerve and finesse to get away with it as convincingly.

British politics is in fact untypical of the rest of society in its adversarial style (symbolism is present in the 'Us and Them' approach to Lower House debate of subjects which, anywhere else, would be treated with much more respect). This confrontational manner is in stark contrast to the consensus-minded approach of the average Briton in his personal life and in business. Fittingly, the links between private sector and government are far less intense in Britain than on the Continent.

73

I believe that many of the charges of hypocrisy brought against the British can be explained by their desire to avoid conflict during discussion or negotiation, a desire that is eventually neutralised by a conviction that 'things have gone too far'. The British back themselves into a corner, then have to fight to get out. Stiff upper lips can lead to bloody noses. A Danish international marketing manager makes the comment that his British salespeople say 'yes' too easily to their customers.

"Forget it"...

No doubt Hofstede can help explain something of the mechanisms underlying British hypocrisy by his conclusion that, next to the Danes, the British come lowest on the European uncertainty avoidance scales together with the Irish. Weak uncertainty avoidance provides a natural breeding ground for eccentricity (for which the British are not always justly famous) and even for a simple and inoffensive desire to appear different.

Eccentricity in turn encourages rhetoric, empty phrases and the like. While foreign business observers politely talk of the British fondness for rhetoric, it often rates as little more than cant. If a British businessman says "very interesting, we'll keep your name on file" or "let's have lunch sometime", more often than not that means "forget it"...

None of this of course is very far removed from that exclusively British and immensely potent phenomenon, class. Of course, the British don't have a monopoly on class (even if they would like to think they do), they just happen to have a particularly insidious and amorphous form of it. Where Continental European class systems tend to operate essentially in terms of education, income, merit and other measurable parameters, the British system factors in subjective things like accent, the way you eat, how you dress, where you come from, and the club you belong to now. It is so subtle that many of its beneficiaries, and even its victims, don't realise what it is doing to them.

Class British-style is also closely linked to a phenomenon which has bedevilled British business for far too long, namely the cult of the amateur, something that has also been called "the contempt of the squirearchy for useful know-ledge." Closely related as it is to the British taste for eccen-tricity, this cult has blossomed since Victorian times. It is strange how Britain revered its engineers in the 19th century (the most famous of whom, Brunel, happened to be a Frenchman), only to treat them with little less than contempt in the 20th. Today, society spurns science as a vocation and British industry shows a marked reluctance to invest in R&D. In the words of *The Economist*: "Under-investing is an age-old British disease."

The dilettante attitude of the British reflects the inborn snobbery of some sections of society as well as a predilec-tion, among those that can afford it, for a liberal education with the emphasis on 'learning the business of life' rather than a vocational one. As *The Economist* says, "Britain's education system undervalues practical skills. This has hit manufacturing hard. The brightest are taught superbly well at university. But those who do not go to university enter the job market with few useful qualifications."

The emergence of what the same magazine called "the plate glass universities" failed to correct this situation by emphasising pure rather than applied subjects, producing more generalists looking for jobs in administration, rather than technically trained engineers or entrepreneurs.

The *International Herald Tribune* asserts that Britain has "fewer business schools and a smaller stock of trained pro-fessional managers than any other European Community nation." But, at the rate they are now spawning, the country must be putting the first of these deficiencies right - if this was in fact the case. Certainly, the academic standards of the top British schools are superior to many of their continental counterparts, and institutions like the London Business School, Warwick, Manchester and Cranfield compare very well with what the rest of Europe has to offer.

Following the publication of the 1971 Bolton Report on the state of British SMEs, the country's business schools invested a lot of money and effort on research into the prin-ciples of entrepreneurship. This was followed by the Thatcher Revolution which, in addition to hastening the destruction of large swathes of traditional industry (not necessarily in itself a bad thing), also encouraged the emergence of a new generation of grassroots businesses which sadly then got knocked on the head by cashflow problems and high interest rates.

British society also encouraged a form of class discrimination, conscious or unconscious, to the detriment not only of engineers, but also of technicians generally and (as in the case of the French) salespeople. Talking to *International Management* magazine Akio Morita, chairman of Sony, expressed his surprise that some British manufacturing companies are led by chief executives "who do not understand the engineering that goes into their own products. This strikes me as very curious..." A researcher, Klaus Schmidt, also found that "some Britons view the process of buying and selling - the very concept embodied in world trade - with misgivings. The visitor who has to come to Britain to

---

Automobile engineering stands out as a striking example of the strengths and weaknesses of British management.

Britain's performance as a mass-producer of cars throughout the 60s and 70s was dismal. A combination of uninspired design, muddled marketing (with a nostalgic attachment to meaningless marques), unduly slow introduction of new manufacturing techniques and poor labour relations ensured the disintegration of what had been a flagship industry - winding up with the British Leyland debacle and the subsequent sale of Rover and Rolls-Royce/Bentley to the Germans.

Yet while all this has been happening small British companies, combining state-of-the-art design and construction technology, have emerged to dominate the Formula One Grand Prix scene.

In 1998, seven of the eleven Grand Prix teams contesting the Grand Prix series – McLaren, Williams, Benetton, Jordan, Stewart, Arrows and Tyrell – were British. Most of the other marques incorporated key components using British technology. Moreover British designed cars and chassis are dominant in the US ' Indy ' and ' Cart ' series.

Those in the know will tell you it all has to do with the British racing tradition and reborn design flair. But it also

---

sell must overcome this attitude." That is very much the attitude of the old school, but it does indeed still persist at some levels of British society.

In stark contrast to both the French and the Germans, the British attachment to the cult of the amateur encourages a mistrust of anyone suspected of precociousness or, funnily enough in the circumstances, overt ambition.

Britain in fact offers more opportunity to the self-taught than an elitist society like France, but there is still a degree of scorn in certain circles towards the 'self-made' man or woman. A recent study by Coopers & Lybrand into British SMEs concluded that, while owner-managers enjoy a position of respect in Germany, their British counterparts - and especially those in manufacturing - do not get the recognition they deserve.

---

has a lot to do with the fact that, individually, the weak-uncertainty-avoidance British love a challenge and, when properly motivated, work superbly well together as a team. In this case, the 'team' concept extends to specialist supplier organisations, also British, most of them located close to the Formula One epicentre in the British Midlands. Shades of Italy (see further on)!

In his book Richard Mead[34] cites the comments of a Californian supplier active in the motor sports arena, explaining the dominance of British teams: "They run like an army... [there is] no time to express our opinions. We have to be very fast, people just have to listen to what they have to do and get on with the job." Mead adds that "the British team works efficiently because the limitations on two-way communication are accepted, and the team refrains from giving feedback to the leader's instructions unless absolutely necessary. They have worked together for some time, and so although each task may consist of a number of stages (and appear complex to a newcomer) it has become routine."

The British have a natural predisposition for teamwork. What a pity that, in the business arena of recent years, they have been so poorly led!

Middle management and manufacturing

The weakest link in the hierarchical chain of British industry has, without question, been its middle management: too many layers, too much meddling, too little real recognition either by senior management or towards the shopfloor. Control is often absent at this intermediate level, in fact much of the inertia of British business may owe its origins to an undue emphasis on titles and 'class distinctions', leading to multiple layers of middle and supervisory management.

In the circumstances it is not surprising that, in 1988, large foreign-owned plants in Britain returned productivity rates 46 per cent higher than those of equivalent British-owned operations. The supportive, 'let's-roll-up-our-sleeves-and-sort-this-out' attitude of Japanese middle management succeeded almost instantly in motivating dour Welsh workers where generations of British managers had failed.

The Economist explains this state of affairs in the following terms: "The British appear to scorn manufacturing. Graduates prefer to become lawyers, financiers or journalists [rather surprisingly, a survey undertaken by the Egon Zehnder consultancy found that the percentage of law graduates was even slightly higher in British than in German top management]. Other studies show that students in Germany are almost four times as likely as British students to consider a career in manufacturing. This cultural bias in Britain against such 'grimy' jobs may just reflect Britain's long-standing comparative advantage in trade, finance and other services (hence higher pay in those areas), or it may be a cause of it."

The rather casual sale of Rover to BMW - dismissive of both the British public and, arguably, the management of Honda - was indicative of this mindset. An opinion piece in the *International Herald Tribune* remarked that "the Rover episode is a telling comment on Britain's disinterest in manufacturing, its complacent belief that it can make a living from services and low-wage industries owned by others."

Despite its rather vicious value system, the City Yuppie generation has indeed shown the country that the British can take business seriously. When they do so, they have unique reserves of creativity and resourcefulness, thanks as much to their weak uncertainty avoidance as anything else. Yet the City is also a culprit in the drama of British decline. Speaking of British 'short-termism' Gottfried Bruder, general manager of the London branch of Commerzbank, says that "the entire financial culture in the UK and its effects on industry are such that, taken together, they constitute a strong disincentive for investment in any form that cannot almost instantly provide returns pleasing to the stock-market." There speaks a German!

On a more positive note, the hallmark of the British mind is pragmatism or, more explicitly, empiricism. In the flux of today's business environment, this characteristic can be helpful in coping with change. Being free of the psychological constraints associated with the highly codified societies of many Continental countries, the British are well equipped to accommodate change - the constant we now have to live with. According to a study undertaken by Jacques Horovitz[21], top British managers give more time to strategic problems than to daily operations: the opposite applies in Germany and France.

This is in stark contrast to the attitudes of the political establishment which reveres pragmatism to the point that 'vision' ranks as a dirty word - along with, to the British, emotive labels like 'bureaucracy', 'federalism' and the like.

Whether the British can exploit the unique opportunity that circumstances now offer them remains to be seen. I have a lingering suspicion that, with their dedication to short-termism, they will let the opportunity pass them by. One international management consultant has said that "the English... are perceived as sociable, flexible and under-prepared..." (two goals minus one own-goal). Another, who works extensively on trilateral British-Dutch-German projects, comments that the British excel themselves as mediators, presenters and after-dinner speakers - having none of the inhibitions of Continentals - but are poor on preparation and often disappointing on follow-up (three goals minus two own-goals).

Yet there could be hope that the British are capable of recovering the entrepreneurial spirit of the Victorians, as evidenced in the uprush of grassroots SMEs in the last few years. The relatively freewheeling behaviour of the average British businessperson, when compared with his or her Continental equivalent, lends itself naturally to such challenging situations. The American in charge of the European subsidiary of a US software company comments that "the British are very creative software designers, but there are always some bugs - we leave it to the tunnel-vision guys to fix them..."

This creativity is also evident in the revitalising impact that the more professional British managers could have, and actually have had, on the life of multinational corporations. Baldwin Klep, a partner with the Heidrick & Struggles executive search consultancy, believes that the British contribution to the present cadre of multinational managers is as important as that of any other country.

Desmond Graves, when examining French organisational behaviour, noted how closely the relationships of French managers conformed to the *organigramme*. He went on to say that British managers, by comparison, cut blithely across the formal lines of command: "patterns of communication bore no relation to the 'official' organization chart." Weak uncertainty avoidance again.

This is, of course, precisely the environment that encourages the ambitious. The CEO referred to above comments rather cruelly: "The trouble is that, now that they no longer have an empire, they all want to build empires of their own." Maybe.

One thing is clear however, namely that there is a world of difference between the traditional British businessman and the younger executives, men and women, rising through the ranks today. There is a new standard of administrative professionalism emerging, still typically pragmatic but more disciplined.

An American CEO running the European end of a multinational business goes so far as to say that the British are the hardest-working and most ambitious of all his subsidiary teams. "They work too much", he complains. "It's not unusual for my UK managing director to call me at 9 o'clock at night (10 o'clock my time) and discuss a problem with me, with all his team present!".

A British consultant, who has lived outside the country for more than 20 years but works regularly for British high-technology corporations, has witnessed the change from an independent standpoint: "The middle management in British hi-tech industries used to be awful: they were poorly educated and poorly motivated. Today people working up the ladder, those in their 40s and early-50s, are far superior in education, ability and performance. They are also harder-working than many Continentals and they certainly work longer hours. But", he adds, "British top management is still too elitist and often amateurish." That word again!

In a Nutshell...

Bosses in **France** tend to be Napoleonic. Graduates as a rule of one of the elite *Grandes Ecoles*, they are expected to be brilliant technical planners, equally adept at industry, finance and government. They can be vulnerable to surprise when troops below fail to respond to orders from on high. Stiff hierarchies in big firms discourage informal relations and reinforce a sense of "them" and "us".

Managers in **Italy** tend to be more flexible. Firms' rules and regulations (where they exist) are often ignored. Informal networks of friends and family contacts matter instead. Decision-making tends to be more secretive than elsewhere, and what goes on in a meeting is often less important than what happens before and after.

This can shock **Germans**, who on the whole prefer to go by the book. Board members tend to have years of technical training and higher degrees. Rarely will a German manager move out of his special field before reaching board-level.

This is in sharp contrast to **Britain**, where tomorrow's top managers tend to be spotted young and then sent rapidly through every department in the firm, giving them a broad, but not always thorough, overview of its operations.

To avoid clashes between these strongly flavoured national cultures, some European countries prefer **Swedish** or **Swiss** chief executives who, it seems, are better blenders.

The Economist

"The Italians work intelligently, simplifying and streamlining concepts and processes. Clever people"

Dutch managing director

"Italians are masters at designing for the market. They have an eye for 'flow', both in design and in business"

American multinational executive

"Sensitive, creative, dynamic"　　　**Danish marketing director**

"I'd prefer to go to work on a donkey. It might improve my image as a charismatic business leader"

Italian condottiere

"The key word in describing the Italian approach and the primary attribute demanded of the manager is 'flexible'

John Mole, *Mind your Manners*

"If you want creative thinking, go to Italy!"

Belgian production director

"Il Dottore è fuori stanza" ["Doctor So-and-So (title obligatory) is not at his desk"]

Popular refrain

"The Italians think being clever is the same thing as being intelligent"

British businessman

"In Italy, everything should change so that nothing will change"

Giuseppe Tomasi di Lampedusa, *The Leopard*

"E se non è vero è ben trovato" ["Even if untrue, it is well found"]

Italian aphorism

ITALY

One of the boasts of the Italians is their individuality: every Italian is a law unto him or herself. They are like all other Europeans in that they adore teamwork when they see it in their footballers but, among themselves, they are less than ideally suited to working together sensibly. Add together their ratings on Hofstede's individualism and masculinity (personal achievement, etc) scales and they come out top, only surpassed by the British (146 against 155).

Yet countless observers, myself included, will tell you that, once they get outside their familiar environment - which of course is Italy or, equally likely, their hometown - Italians stick together more hermetically than any other European nationality with the exception of the Albanians.

In fact there are some striking situations in business where Italians show a sense of common purpose which is as dramatic and as effective as anything you will find elsewhere. I am thinking of the grassroots movements that have emerged - not just the agricultural and wine producing cooperatives that have taken much of Europe by storm, but also the regional industries that owe their success to intelligent and neighbourly cooperation.

Examples are the automotive and engineering component suppliers around Bologna, the specialised steel makers of Brescia, the textile firms of Prato and Biella, the tilemakers of Sassuolo and Reggio Emilia, the furniture manufacturers of Pesaro, the shoemakers of Vigevano, and the domestic appliance manufacturers of eastern and northeastern Italy. Nothing quite like this exists anywhere else in Europe, except for some of the small and specialised industries to be found, for example, in Swabia, in the north of Spain and in the British Midlands (see page 77).

This reflects the hallmark of Italian society, the principle of the 'extended family'. Its bedrock is indeed the family, however modest (and paradoxically diminishing), but it extends from there into the immediate circle of distant relatives and close friends and, from there, into the principle of *lottizazione* ('jobs for the boys'), which is not yet dead and, from there, into The Family itself. This degree of networking - which includes affiliations to cooperatives, trades unions and political parties - was perfected millenia before the Americans reinvented the word and is both the great strength and the weakness of Italian society.

One inevitable aspect of networking is the 'jobs for the boys' syndrome, for which Italy has been rightly famous - although vigorously challenged by its Mediterranean neighbours and some other countries to the north. In his book *The Italians*[22] Luigi Barzini speaks of *sistemazione*, the dream of most Italians: "It does not necessarily signify hard work, responsibility, good wages, and the possibility of getting ahead, but often nothing more than a mediocre but durable position, protected from unseen events, with a predictable career, some moral authority, and a pension at the end." Plus the opportunity to moonlight on the side.

Stuart Miller, in his book *Painted in Blood*[23], reports that "70 percent of the generation of Italy's famous economic boom, the kids born between 1960 and 1965, albeit coming on the labour market during a time of national budgetary cutbacks, have the following aspiration: they want to find a *posto fisso*, a permanent government job, the kind that cannot by law ever be cut from any budget, even if society doesn't need it anymore."

Maybe the emergence of the new post-*Tangentopoli* ('Kickback City') Italy will change all this, but I doubt it. The syndrome is deeply embedded in the Italian psyche and, in any case, as John Mole points out, "only one in five employees are in public service occupations as opposed to just over one in three in the UK and just under one in three in the USA and Germany."

Clannishness, or the technique of the extended family, is to some extent a device to counter innate insecurity. In international gatherings, the Italians are remarkable for keeping very much to themselves, even more than the Germans or the Swedes. The Spanish by comparison - in stark contrast to the stereotype of the proud, distant *hidalgo* - are much less exclusive in their relationships.

Inevitably clannishness has a geographical dimension. Current politics clearly highlights the rift between the mainly industrialised North and the mainly agrarian South, the Mezzogiorno. As John Mole says: "The two regions have markedly different attitudes to life and business. The stereotypical northerner is preoccupied with work and money, the southerner with power and the good life."

In fact there are a myriad of micro-faultlines within Italian society, both horizontally between different families and factions, and vertically between different regions and towns. The spirit of localism goes back to the mediaeval Italy of the city states, when even town districts had their own cheerleaders and regalia, fuelling people's sense of local identity like today's football teams. Today, in addition to football teams, it survives in phrases like '*Torinese, freddo e cortese*' and in the northerner's anxiety to dissociate himself from his car's Roman numberplates...

Insecurity, the Italian *leitmotiv*, inevitably engenders - in addition to clannishness - suspicion of anything or anyone unknown. A characteristic of Italian business is the excessive importance attached to secrecy or confidentiality of information when compared with most other European countries. Mistrust, sometimes of fellow-Italians but particularly of foreigners, is widespread as I have found out to my cost. Using a camera in a manufacturing plant to take totally innocent shots of a supplier's equipment is instantly identified as industrial espionage.

Suspicion is also directed as a matter of principle at all forms of officialdom, from the local tax office to national government, even when they offer the hope of favours or employment.

A more surprising expression of insecurity, in the opinion of Luigi Barzini, is the Italian's search for symmetry. This, fortuitously, not only produces some of the finest design standards the world has to offer, it also encourages a sense of perfectionism. I know of an Italian machinery importer who found the wide tolerances practised by his American suppliers so offensive that he had their machines recalibrated at his own cost.

Another design-related phenomenon is also evident in the new upwardly mobile classes, who exploit the Italian penchant for theatricality and the *bella figura*: the men wear designer-everything, including mobile phones, and the women go skiing in furcoats.

Getting round the system

Understandably, the Italian business world was destabilised by developments in the opening years of the 1990s, first the devaluation of the lire, then the *Tangentopoli* scandal and its *mani puliti* ('clean hands') sequel. Most companies decided not to invest or to make strategic decisions - something that doesn't come very easily to Italian businesspeople in any case - until the dust had died down.

Italy's wealth is without question its human skills, practical, intellectual and entrepreneurial. Unfortunately, the expressions of industriousness and creativity that have attracted the most attention in the media in recent years are ones which do little credit to the skills involved.

Even Italian industry has directed much of its efforts to getting round the system, to the extent that the true wealth of Italy is undervalued - until the country makes another of its startling economic recoveries. As an Italian businessman said, with a typically disarming turn of phrase: "Other Western economies are like battleships, beautifully constructed but easily torpedoed. The Italian economy is a raft - and how do you sink a raft?" He omitted to mention the *economia sommersa*, the bit underneath. Indeed much of Italian industry, particularly the SME sector, is built essentially for survival - and, on the evidence of the squalls and seachanges it has gone through, it is robustly constructed.

Outside the SMEs, the Italian industrial scene has until recently been characterised by a lumbering state sector, now in the process of privatisation, and an elite group of mainly family-owned large firms in the private sector: industrial landmarks like Fiat, Olivetti, Pirelli, Ferruzzi, Ligresti and more recent and highly successful ventures like Benetton. Essentially Italian manufacturing is an engineering culture.

Each of these companies has its own character. A British consultant says that the difference in culture between Fiat and Olivetti is enormous, even though they're only 100 kilometers apart. While Fiat is traditionally very production-oriented, there are important functional cultures creating faultlines within it and other large Italian companies, particularly between engineers on the one hand and marketing/sales people on the other.

Clearly the dominance of the *condottieri*-led companies is in question. Despite their membership of a cosy inner sanctum dubbed the *salotto buono*, the barons of Italian big business have habitually made a mess of things internationally in recent years. De Benedetti's abortive raid on the Belgian Société Générale was followed by Leopoldo Pirelli's frustrated takeover of Germany's Continental tyremaker and, more recently, by Gianni Agnelli's ill-fated bid for the French Perrier group.

While there are a lot of lessons to be learned from all three escapades about the business cultures of the target countries - Belgium, Germany and France - they also tell you something about the Italians: an insouciance about the psychology of the other party, an element of Latin pride, and a stubbornness in persisting in the wrong approach.

Indeed the days of Italy's industrial dynasties may be numbered. Foreign multinationals are rapidly dominating important sectors of the Italian economy. Companies controlled by the Swedish Wallenberg organisation comprise the second largest industrial group in Italy. Pharmacia & Upjohn not long ago acquired Farmitalia/Carlo Erba. And, despite the fame of native brands like Barilla and Buitoni, even the top spots in Italy's food industry are occupied by names like Nestlé, Unilever, BSN and Kraft Jacob Suchard.

Professionalism, not patronage

Thanks to the efforts of a number of university-linked business schools, notably the SDA Bocconi in Milan, a new generation of managers is emerging which is more interested in professionalism than patronage. The Egon Zehnder survey referred to earlier found that the percentages of Italian managers with degrees in economics, natural sciences and engineering were more or less equal, but that there were far fewer lawyers than in either Germany or Britain.

Management structures and techniques vary widely, depending on the size and to some extent the location of the company concerned. John Mole, writing in 1990 (lightyears away in terms of Italian current affairs), summed up life in the larger organisations in the following words: "In large companies a conventional hierarchy in the sense of clear reporting lines from superior to subordinate [or the other way round?] is only to be found at the lower levels of the organisation. At middle to upper levels the true hierarchies are built on personal alliances between people in different parts of the organisation who trust each other and rely on each other to get things done."

"There is a strong and growing professional class in the private sector", Mole explains. "It is especially active in private companies which have outgrown their original family based structures. Thirty years ago a talented graduate would go into the public sector. Now the status, pay and opportunities are in the private sector even for a person with no direct connections."

Where John Mole talks about a flexible attitude to decision-making, many Italian managers would readily admit to opportunism. "There is a keen entrepreneurial sense based on recognition of new opportunities in the market. Italian companies thrive on ambiguity and risk."

This opportunism is closely related to creativity. The technical director of a Belgian multinational says: "The Italians are the most creative thinkers I know, the best 'developers' in Europe. If I had a real problem, I could always rely on them to brainstorm and come up with an answer. But at the same time, you have to keep them on the rails. Sometimes they get so enthused with an idea that they ignore the hard facts."

A Swedish DP manager confirms that his Italian team are much faster in planning and implementing new computer systems than their opposite numbers in his German subsidiary. You can understand why when you hear the comments made by an Olivetti executive to Samuel Humes: "A little chaos is seen as necessary to maintain an innovative environment. Rules and regulations inhibit creativity so the challenge is to manage this chaos sufficiently to avoid anarchy." Management Italian-style!

One characteristically assertive Israeli managing director I talked to was in no doubt as to the qualities of the Italians he had to deal with, mainly in the printing and publishing trades in the north, when he was running his company's Italian subsidiary. "They are very business-oriented and ded-

90

icated people", he insists, "they understand what you mean very quickly and they use their time intelligently."

"Moreover, they're not lazy, they just do things faster and take time off if they want to. They can also be extraordinarily helpful and honest: because of a misunderstanding, I lost money on a deal and they gave it back! For me, they combine in one people all the best of Europe: efficiency, creativity and warmth."

While the *condottieri* stumble, Italy's SMEs, mainly concentrated in the North, go on squirrelling away in the economic undergrowth to enormous effect. Italian SMEs, unlike the SMEs of many other European countries, are entrepreneurial, innovative and risk-taking. Benetton, which rose out of the SME ranks, is a perfect example.

Without question it is the SMEs that are the white hope of Italian industry (businesses with less than 100 employees produced 87 per cent of Italy's GNP in 1993!). As non-quoted companies, mainly family businesses or cooperatives, they are the spine of the economy, combining enough strength with enough flexibility to survive the worst that can happen to them and their country. Their role in the Italian economy and society owes a lot to the traditional scenario painted and promoted by the Christian Democrat party which, at the same time as propping up (and preying on) state industries, favoured the family enterprise.

The proprietor of the average Italian SME is totally unmoved by what the rest of the world thinks, but also in the sense that Italian medium size businesses are the most, if not almost the only, dynamic element in the Italian economy. Here the profile of the 'classical' SME is determined not by social attitudes but by the imperative of avoiding giving more away than necessary, money or information. When you are small, you can rely on outworkers and self-employed personnel, you can pay cash and keep your social charges and your tax bill to a minimum. Moreover, companies employing under 200 people enjoy exemption from the disclosure rules that are supposed to govern Italian big business.

The result is that, as soon as a company hits this ceiling, it spawns off a separate enterprise with which it has no

91

apparent official links. A Dutch international businessman recounts the case of an Italian SME he has dealings with which decentralised its engineering department, while retaining financial control, by literally 'farming out' work: he found a new product development unit in the farmyard barn of one of the company's employees.

That is clearly taking things to their limits, unless one thinks of the ceramics factory near Rome that was mounted on wheels to evade the tax collector. But, in its more responsible guise, this Italian SME spawning process has produced a series of incubator environments, many of them anchored in specific locations, which are the modern-day equivalent of the guilds and artisan industries of the mediaeval Italian city-states.

No one has developed the contractor/subcontractor relationship to a finer art than the Italians, with companies like Benetton putting work out to a wide circle of *appaltatori*. The extended family again!

There are also signs that Italy's family firms are growing up. The new generation of sons and daughters, stepping into the shoes of founder-fathers who generally pioneered their companies in the years after World War II, is better educated, often fluent in foreign languages and, as a result, much more cosmopolitan in outlook. If these youngsters apply the same entrepreneurial flair internationally that their parents applied at home in the past, Italian business will be a major player in the European Single Market.

Leadership Excellence in Europe

In 1997 PA Consulting Group, in association with the Aarhus School of Business of Denmark, polled the opinions of over 200 senior management executives in the UK, Germany, France, the Benelux countries and Denmark on their individual leadership styles. Most of them were nationals of the countries in which they worked.

The study matched responses against a profile of the components essential to business excellence, embodying the three key principles of Total Quality Management (TQM), Creativity and Learning. These components were: a focus on customers and their needs; continuous improvement; the empowerment and participation of all staff members; a focus on facts; a commitment to creativity; and an orientation towards continuous learning. Some of these components - as will be evident from Chapter 5, page 223 *et seq* - do not blend so well with the cultures of the European south.

The researchers identified eight different management styles, none of which was exclusive and all of which might be present, in varying degrees, in the same person. These styles were:

The Captain : commands respect and trust, leads from the front, professionally competent, communicative, reliable and fair.

The Creative leader: innovative, visionary, courageous, inspiring, strong sense of ego.

The Involved leader: empathises, a 'hands-on' approach, does not delegate, focuses on procedures.

The Task leader: analytical, 'bottom-line'-driven, result-oriented, impersonal, persevering, intolerant of mistakes.

The Strategic leader: focuses on strategic goals, takes

a holistic view of the organisation, a good planner, avoids day-to-day detail, process-oriented, trustworthy.

The Impulsive leader: obsessed with new ideas, unfocused, curious, energetic, participative.

The Specialist leader: expert, solitary, lacks inspirational ability, resistant to change, calm.

The Team Builder leader: tolerant, gives feedback, acts as a coach, motivates, inspires, supportive.

While the overall results show that most European top managers still have a lot to learn about leadership excellence, regardless of age, there are some significant variations in the emphasis different cultures place on the different components of managerial competence. The results also show that many of the respondents know themselves well and, maybe without realising it, are honest about their inclinations.

For example, the French come across as very much oriented toward the Creative Leadership style ('visionary', 'strong sense of ego', etc) whereas the Danes clearly favour the Impulsive approach. Both fit with the conclusions reached in this book. The Germans, who come out closest to the ideal of Leadership Excellence in this study by scoring high in terms of both Strategic thinking and Task orientation, also stand out in the Specialist category. No surprises there either.

It is also interesting to compare the results of this study with the conclusions of the Cranfield Executive Competencies Survey on page 204. The only problem I have with the present study is the use of 'Benelux' as a category. There are in my opinion still too many differences between the management styles of the Dutch and the Belgians - let alone between the Flemish and the Walloons - to make this meaningful.

'Achieving Business Excellence: Successful Leadership Styles', PA Consulting Group, 1997

"Ambitious people. They want to get ahead, make better products. Very realistic"
American multinational executive

"A new Spanish character, one that contradicts all the past images, is just being defined. At the moment we are almost infantile in our enthusiasm and vitality, and have trouble defining ourselves"
Ernesto Ekaizer, *Cinco Dias*

"For a Spaniard, success lies in the title as much as in the salary, and much more than in the work"
Helen Wattley Ames, *Spain is Different*

"The importance of personal contacts is well known wherever people of the Spanish race are concerned. Whether the question in debate is a trivial affair or of the most important business, a relation of man to man is indispensable if results are to be obtained"
Salvador de Madariaga

"We Spaniards appreciate spontaneity and someone who is simpático - *the personal approach is all-important"*
Spanish businessman

"The ideal leader is a benevolent autocrat... The quality most admired in a leader is to be courageous - valiente*"*
John Mole, speaking about the Spanish

"Spain's problem is that the model of life today is the speculator"
Primitivo Gurpegui

"Competitiveness, in particular, is associated with envidia, *the Spanish vice"*
Helen Wattley Ames, *Spain is Different*

"The idea that companies are objects bought and sold by powerful people in furtherance of their own ends is consistent with the Spanish corporate culture"
Tom Lloyd, *The European*

"I'm sorry to say there are signs they are more corruptible than I thought"
Belgian marketing director

SPAIN

The Spanish as a people suffer from an image problem, having retired from world domination to turn their backs on the rest of Europe. The 'Generation of '98' (nb 1898) triggered a process that brought them back to their senses, but the process was only completed with the demise of the Franco regime.

But much of the image problem is of other peoples' making and therefore particularly difficult to eradicate. The French artistic stereotypes that people the plot of 'Carmen' and other romantic essays are much closer to the gypsies than they are to the sturdy and matter-of-fact mentality of most Spaniards. On top of this many people still today graft on the 'sombrero and poncho' images associated with films about Mexican bandits (who seem to spend a lot of their time, hats tilted over, asleep in the sun). This has been reinforced by false impressions of Spain brought back by holidaymakers who only know the concrete-and-plastic coastal resorts and are totally unaware of the real Spain of the interior.

All of this does great injustice to the Spaniards and, by implication to Spanish business. The reality is rather different.

'Reality' is a good word to start with for, whatever else, Spanish businesspeople are realists, though you will still find the odd Don Quixote who lives, at least part of the time, a life of fantasy. A philosophical disposition is common to many Spaniards, and not just the educated classes, and can lead to verbal long-windedness and a habit of saying the same thing a number of ways (*'o sea... o sea'*) to be sure you've got the point.

The Spanish also have a natural sense of equality, the very thing their French neighbours seem to lack. With the French the concept is cerebral, with the Spanish it is visceral. It might be more apt to describe this sense of equality as a 'sense of fellowship'. By comparison, intelligence *per se* has a much lower rating with the Spanish than with the French.

In business dealings, this sentiment often expresses itself in a rather old-worldly 'grand manner' based on mutual respect. This appeal to a mutual sense of honour may seem a bit far-fetched to cynical foreigners, but it is mostly genuinely felt and does all concerned credit: the Spanish do

99

indeed want to be perceived as honourable people (though they have their fair share of business corruption) and are happy to treat you in the same way. Relationships are often intimate and lasting.

As an example of this sense of honour, I offer the story of a Spanish company which, having committed itself to engaging a recruit and then confronted with evidence of the candidate's unsuitability, felt constrained to hire him on probation until the company could prove that he was unsuited to the job - and fired him six months later!

Inevitably, conservatism is a related trait, particularly in the older generation. It also reflects, in all generations, a natural sense of caution: the Spanish lie fairly high on Hofstede's uncertainty avoidance scale.

This conservatism is evident in both manner and dress: appearance is more important in Spain than in many other Continental countries including France. In a business meeting in Valencia with a group of directors of family businesses, I was reminded of nothing less than the affability and decorum of a London Club. There are surprising overtones of the British way of life. Unfortunately the flashy tie and furcoat brigade are moving in. Posh offices are also increasingly *de rigueur*.

Natural dignity can easily be interpreted as pride, a quality that Spaniards possess, but that is sometimes made too much of by foreigners. Despite innate self-esteem, Spaniards demonstrate a high degree of circumspection, even modesty, in their dealings with others. But some Spaniards, particularly the older generations, seem to use pride as a preemptive stance to conceal a totally unjustified inferiority complex vis-a-vis other European cultures.

The latter is the result of a very long period of history which started with the disintegration of the Spanish Empire and ended with the decision to join the European Union as the poor supplicant. It takes no account of the enormous progress, both social and economic, made since. But, if the Spanish have anything to match the inner tensions evident in other European cultures, the 'psycho-poles' I have talked about elsewhere, you will probably find it here.

It also takes time for a society to come to terms with the rest of a continent that it had so studiously turned its back on for so many centuries. Spaniards still have a tendency to dismiss the opinions of others, particularly if they are foreigners, and to dislike them heartily if they turn out to be right!

In his book *The Spaniard and the Seven Deadly Sins*[24], Fernando Diaz-Plaja says: "The way to improve the Spaniard can be summed up in a possibility as simple as it is revolutionary. If from time to time, only from time to time, we were to believe that the other man might be right... And if this belief did not automatically make him odious... I believe that would be enough."

Envy, of course, was one of the seven deadly sins. And envy has long been regarded by others, not entirely with justification in my opinion, as one of the *leitmotifs* of Spanish culture at the personal level. In professional life it helps explain the fragility of the Spanish business community today. In the words of a Spanish journalist and businessman, "the cult of individualism expresses itself in jealousy and rejection of those who are successful." The result is a philosophy of 'if you can't beat them, despise them', a philosophy that has gained ground with the overall increase in wealth. "As long as people were poor, they knew better!"

This attitude may to some extent be explained by a natural reluctance to compete. As Helen Wattley Ames explains in her book *Spain is Different*[25]: "In the Spanish work environment competitiveness is seen as negative whenever it interferes with good working relationships. People are not expected to compete openly for preference or advancement."

Envy may also now play a part in the perceived overlap in the Spanish mind between service and servility. Though I have had plenty of experiences to the contrary, more and more people - Spanish and foreigners - maintain that Spaniards increasingly demonstrate an inability to cope with the demands of the service-industry age: the explosive mixture of dignity with a dash of envy inhibits them in being helpful to others.

In the words of Salvador de Madariaga[26]: "The instinct for preserving his own liberty makes him [the Spaniard] eschew

101

all forms of social co-operation, since all collective work tends to enslave the individual and to reduce him to the status of a piece of machinery." This view was even being voiced as long ago as 1836, when George Borrow encountered an innkeeper in Valladolid who was "far too high a cavalier to attend to the wants of his guests."

A market researcher friend of mine maintains, from extensive dealings with the Spanish business community, that they combine the rigidity of the Germans with the apparent self-assurance of the British (I use the word 'apparent' advisedly). One thing is for sure. The Spanish can be both dynamic and inventive, and are currently showing the rest of Europe a thing or two. Some engineering companies - particularly Basque ones, the Basques producing brilliant engineers - are as good as anything Europe can offer. In fact engineering enjoys as exalted a status as in France, possibly more so. Spanish non-technical design - styling and graphics - is also improving rapidly, to the point that it now challenges the standards of the frontrunner, Italy.

The lack of an entrepreneurial tradition

Spain only committed itself morally to a European future with Franco's demise in 1975. So it is hardly surprising that, with currency controls and industries essentially serving the domestic market, there was little incentive for the country to breed a class of professional managers of international calibre. Moreover, much of industry was privately owned or propped up by the state.

The situation was not helped by the fact that Spanish society traditionally showed little interest in or enthusiasm for business, echoing British attitudes. In the words of Carlos Caballé, dean of the IESE (Instituto de Estudios Empresariales), the country's leading management school: "Spain lacks an entrepreneurial tradition. Until recently Spaniards did not look favourably upon people who started their own businesses and made profits." Rather like the situation in both Britain and Germany until recently...

José Luis Alvarez, a professor at IESE, goes so far as to say that "in Spain, business ideas, even economic values in general, have been despised for centuries." A Danish multinational VP who runs a manufacturing and sales operation in Spain confirms this from his personal experience: "Spanish business society is developing, but not as fast as I would have hoped. There is not enough local talent."

Reflecting these public prejudices, the profession *par excellence* as in France and Germany has been engineering, which conferred a status and allure that totally outshone the practice of making money - and this in a country that traditionally spurned earthly values in any case!

A study undertaken among European top managers in 1991 by the Egon Zehnder International executive search firm showed that, while lawyers were much less in evidence than in Germany and the UK, 57 per cent of Spanish respondents had engineering degrees. Indeed some regions of Spain - the Basque Provinces and Catalonia in particular - are renowned for their engineering skills. The same study also showed that the age profile of Spanish managers differed from that of the more mature European economies: the average age was 48 years compared with 50+ elsewhere, and 13 per cent of Spanish managers were under 40 years.

Spain has three important business schools: IESE and ESADE in Barcelona, and the Instituto de Empresa in Madrid. The country is taking a growing interest in management education. Teaching methods are becoming more interactive, though the younger generation of Spaniards seems to display an untypical reluctance to challenge or debate the ideas put to it.

Like Germany, Spain is a country where regional differences count for a lot. The current reality can be summed up by thinking of Spain in terms of three large areas, two of which are troubled economically, the third still flourishing.

The first area comprises the northwestern provinces of Asturias and Guipuzcoa, where the actions of ETA terrorists have hampered new investment in what is rapidly becoming a rustbelt. The second comprises Andalusia, Spain's most densely populated province, and Estremadura which, in the words of a Catalan journalist, enjoy a 'sunshine and castanets culture' allied with uncompetitive wages. Happily the third area, the Mediterranean coast from the French frontier to Alicante, combines a more dynamic industrial culture (including a number of major US multinational implants) with a thriving agro-industry and tourism. There are also important industrial concentrations around Madrid, particularly hi-tech companies, and Saragossa (chemicals, automobiles, etc).

The mentalities of the regions, like their climates and landscapes, also differ dramatically. The people of the northwest have a matter-of-fact business approach which contrasts starkly with the Mediterranean trading style of the Catalans in the northeast. Yet the latter tend to be much more open and direct than the archetypal Castilian Spaniard, and they come across as particularly astute businesspeople. As a British manager who has also dealt widely in the Middle East put it to me: "You can only do business with the Catalans if you're prepared to lose money!"

In matters other than trading, the Catalans come off worse. In a paper entitled 'Regional Cultures, Managerial Behavior and Entrepreneurship: an International Perspective', Nieves Martinez and Pedro Nueno sum up Catalan cultural traditions as "stubborn individualism, lack of trust to delegate responsibility to high caliber managers, overreliance on family members and unprofessional 'trust-men' [a traditional feature of Spanish business]; the tendency to consistently underinvest; the diversion of a large percentage of revenue to unrelated core business activities; and inattention to resupplying equipment (keeping equipment beyond obsolescence)." Sounds much like SME attitudes elsewhere.

Industry, bureaucracy, bankers, church...

The Spanish business scene still has to develop the clear contours of other European economies. The air of novelty it enjoys is reflected in the public attention focused on certain public figures who, in recent years, have been the subject of sensationalist treatment in the popular press. In the words of José Luis Alvarez of IESE, "among the 'beautiful people', businessmen, usually from the finance sector, are prominent (several very publicized sexual affairs helped that along). Also prominent in the press is a new cohort of young bankers that have arrived at the top of their organizations, substituting the traditional gerontocracy of the Spanish banking sector."

Yet some features are evident enough. First there is INI, the state industrial holding company, which has played an important role in developing a new business elite favoured by the government (rather in the same way as the French *Ministère des Finances*). Socialist patronage, not content with 'jobs for the boys', extended to placing people on company boards and contributed to the emergence of a new middle class.

Second, there are the family banking dynasties, which still pull many of the strings in Spain's industrial complex (begging comparison with the role of Germany's banks) and, third, a much maligned organisation called the Opus Dei.

The private banking families are still Spain's most powerful single lobby. The traditional banking dynasties, the *banqueros*, have been joined since the demise of the Franco regime by an upstart group of self-made bankers, the *bancarios*, of whom the best known for the wrong reasons is Mario Conde. Between them they control important segments of Spanish business through third-party holdings, 'front' companies and the like.

The Opus Dei - a practically minded and highly motivated arm of the Roman Catholic church yet a distinctly Spanish creation - plays a discreet background role in business. Its aim is to extend Christian precepts to everyday life, appealing to employers and employees alike. It has its adherents throughout industry, particularly in the SME sector, in agriculture and in the banking community, as well as in academia (the University of Navarra).

The organisation has friends among the Spanish business and academic elite, who support it as a moral preceptor and as a stabilising influence within society. Adherents included Alberto Ullastres and Lopez Rodó, ministers in the 1957 cabinet that set Spain on the road to modernisation. Because it is secretive, slightly elitist and very successful, the Opus Dei tends to have the same image with non-Catholics as the masonic lodges have with Catholics.

Spanish businesspeople, like every other business community in Europe, have their 'old boy' network which, in their case, runs under the name of *enchufismo*. All the above, starting with the socialists, are major components of this club. Another component is Spanish bureaucracy which presents the average citizen with a permanent challenge: how to get round the system? As Helen Wattley Ames points out, "there is a proverb [Spaniards are strong on proverbs], *Hecha la ley, hecha la trampa*, which means 'Every law has its loophole'..."

Outside these distinct constituencies - the INItes, banking, Opus Dei, SMEs and bureaucrats - the Spanish business scene is diffuse. SMEs predominate, big business is the exception rather than the rule, and there are in effect no Spanish multinationals (those that purport to be are boasting). As in other Latin countries, big business tends to be bureaucratic, small business autocratic.

In *Mind your Manners*, John Mole comments that "a traditional style of Spanish management is found in family companies, large state-owned companies and some of the older established multinationals with Spanish management. They tend to be run on highly compartmentalised, bureaucratic and authoritarian lines. The introduction of, primarily, American management methods and the attitudes to authority among younger people brought up in the new political climate often generates conflict and stress between generations."

Yet, compared with many other European countries, Spanish youth is relatively docile. Speaking of the younger generation, a Spanish manager says: "If you scratch the surface of most of them, you will find that they are very timid - the machismo talk is just a cover-up."

The extended family syndrome fostered by the Italians is also much in evidence in Spain. Gerald Brenan helps explain Spanish business relationships when commenting on social attitudes in his book *The Face of Spain*[27]: "The whole of Spanish life, one may say, is organized in a sort of clan system. Within the clan - which consists of relatives, friends, political allies, and so forth - all is warmth and friendliness: outside it all is distrust and suspicion." As Helen Wattley Ames says, "family support extends into professional as well as personal life." Despite the spirit of egalitarianism, the social classes are still clearly defined: "It would be unheard of for a person from the middle class to

take such jobs as delivering newspapers or waiting tables...
In Spanish corporations, the higher echelons are still filled
to a great extent by the upper class."

Spain's SMEs, the dominating feature of the country's
economy, suffer from being remote from Europe's main markets and, partly because of this, from a lack of opportunity
to develop their self-confidence. Their most spectacular representatives are the series of businesses that have developed
around the Mondragon cooperative in the Basque provinces,
a phenomenon which bears comparison with the *Bresciani*
and others in Italy.

Unfortunately, their example is not followed throughout
Spain. Speaking of Estremadura and Andalusia, a Spanish
minister of industry was heard to comment that "you can't
do anything with them..." And even when the engineering
skills exist, there is insufficient awareness of disciplines like
quality management. As *The Economist* says: "Despite
recent improvements, Spanish component makers are still
famous for *chapuzas* (botched jobs)."

So there is good and bad in Spanish business, as everywhere.

"The Dutch occupy one of the world's most densely populated countries, and they structure life in it by means of a seemingly irrevocable commitment to a meticulously detailed but at the same time flexible system of interlocking organization"

William Z Shetter

"While the Germans are busy perfecting the past, the Dutch are focusing on the future"

British marketing consultant

"There are two cultures in The Netherlands: the official one as evident in the democratic process, education and so on, and a subculture which doesn't respect these things"

Dutch managing director

"The Dutch tend to disregard the opinions of 'outsiders'. If you're a foreigner and a woman, it's worse. And if you insist, they say 'don't get emotional'"

Belgian woman executive

"When asked to tackle an intellectual task for a business plan, the Dutch draw organisation charts"

British marketing consultant

"The Dutch are traditionally introverted and cautious, but extremely well educated, intelligent and ready to learn..."

Belgian CEO of Dutch subsidiary

"Je moet plannen om met een taxi te gaan, maar je gaat toch met de fiets" ["You should plan to go by taxi, but still take your bike"]

Dutch saying

"In matters of commerce, the fault of the Dutch is offering too little and asking too much"

George Canning, British Foreign Secretary, in a ciphered dispatch to Sir Charles Bagot, English Ambassador at The Hague, 31 January 1826

HOLLAND

While presenting a sturdily cohesive image to the outside world, the Dutch culture is highly complex in terms of both social structure and the makeup of the individual Dutch mind. Even its identity is complex. Many people, myself included, say 'Holland' when we should be saying 'The Netherlands'. Holland is only part of the country, the part that feeds the stereotype images of cheese, clogs and women with rearview mirrors. And while the slang word in Dutch for 'business' does happen to be *kaas* (cheese), there's a lot more to The Netherlands than that.

The culture, which to unsuspecting foreigners looks monolithic, is made up of a number of components. The most evident of these historically are the *zuilen*, or 'pillars', representing various streams of politico-religious (or irreligious) thought: Roman Catholic, Orthodox Reformed (Calvinist), Reformed (Calvinist) and other Protestant, Socialist, and General and Non-church. Their influence on Dutch society between the 1930s and the 1960s was such that they still mark various facets of Dutch life today.

As for the individual Dutch mind it reveals, like the mindsets of many other European cultures, an inherent tension between opposing values, another set of 'psycho-poles'. In the words of a British marketing consultant who has lived and worked many years in The Netherlands: "The Dutch have a traditionally very conformist society, even if they claim to be pluralistic."

A clear insight into this dilemma is provided by the author Simon Schama[28] when he talks about the classic Dutch counterpoint between materialism and morality. He speaks of "...the moral geography of the Dutch mind, adrift between the fear of the deluge and the hope of moral salvage, in the tidal ebb and flow between worldliness and homeliness, between the gratification of appetite and its denial, between the conditional consecration of wealth and perdition in its surfeit." No wonder the Dutch can be people of extremes, despite their professions to the contrary!

Such was the moral conflict within Dutch society at the height of the country's power: that so small a community had such an influence on world affairs is remarkable. It may be this achievement, added to the inner tensions, that produced the present-day contradictions in the Dutch character, in particular the to-and-fro between social conformity and individual assertiveness. The democratic Dutch can be excessively dogmatic.

This comes out in the comments of many international businesspeople who have dealings with the Dutch. Their close neighbours in particular find the Dutch mentality irksome. "In discussions they can be rude out of what seems to me like arrogance", says a Belgian architect. "They are sometimes so uncompromising that they destroy relationships and, thereby, any hope of finding a satisfactory solution." But, the Dutch would say, there speaks a Belgian!

One side-effect of the democratic upbringing practised in The Netherlands is a reluctance to show off in public. This can have some funny effects on the behaviour of Dutch businesspeople in a corporate environment (see Chapter 4), whether they are dealing with their fellow-executives or with outsiders. But it is particularly perplexing for foreigners who, having adjusted to this degree of modesty, are then astonished to be moralised at. Despite their democratic upbringing, the Dutch are just as capable of bragging as any of the other Europeans, maybe even more so.

Moralising and meticulousness

The moralising tendency should not be taken too seriously: it is meant with the best intentions and is as often directed at their fellows as much as at foreigners. As one of their number puts it, "we have a tendency to lecture, preach and teach on any subject that is not our business" (some people say that, with foreigners, they just say what the latter want to hear).

The writer J van Laarhoven describes The Netherlands as "a country... of practical tolerance and impractical pedantry." No wonder the English say that 'he talked like a Dutch uncle': the moralising streak is highly developed. An eminent sociologist put it in blander terms: "We Dutch think helping is important, as long as we're not on the receiving end..."

Closely linked to the moralising trait is a tendency to look, and occasionally be, genuinely tightfisted. The meanness of the Dutch is one of the most durable European stereotypes and not without reason. I prefer to describe this mindset as 'frugality' - there is no point in spending money unnecessarily.

By definition this should qualify the Dutch as good businesspeople, as long as they're running their own affairs. Indeed, thanks to their mercantile history, they qualify as some of Europe's most astute traders, in fact they have the rare distinction of being both skilful traders and good marketers, unlike the Belgians and the Greeks. The trading instinct is still very much in evidence in some segments of Dutch society (see below).

But when the Dutch attribute their appreciation of the value of money to foreigners, or even in some cases to their fellow-Dutchmen, they may be assuming too much. A number of major consumer marketing fiascos can be traced back to underestimation by Dutch managers of the ability of their compatriots to pay more for better quality. By aspiring to perfection, at a price, Dutch marketers end up with mediocrity.

Yet, get the better of their instincts, and Dutch marketers can be excellent. The Finnish marketing director of a major multinational says that, of all his country teams, "the Dutch are the best at adding value to cost, they manage to sell the same product for a higher price than anyone else."

Cautious with money, the Dutch also pay careful attention to detail. Many people comment on their meticulousness, the way they 'go by the book'. To the Dutch this is only natural, to some foreigners it looks like stubbornness. The British marketing consultant referred to above says that the Dutch concentrate on detail to the extent that they sometimes "miss the big picture".

This may also have something to do with the fact that, in the minds of some Dutch executives, delegation amounts to nothing less than handing total responsibility for a task to a subordinate. The boss washes his hands of the job, neither briefing the wretched individual nor expecting feedback.

The same marketing consultant suggests that attention to detail may be motivated in part by dislike of criticism: "they try to make sure that whatever they do is perfect." Perhaps for this reason even the Belgians agree that the Dutch make excellent middle management material. It may also explain why they can be so critical of others. The production director of a major Belgium-based multinational with Dutch subsidiaries comments that "I have to demonstrate I have a right to be the boss every time."

This meticulousness of the Dutch, with regard both to detail and to money, is an admirable business quality as long as it is channelled in the right way. Being a people of intermittent extremes - despite their professed addiction to the middle of the road - they tend to let this quality get out of hand. Seen from the viewpoint of their closest neighbours, the expansive and 'Burgundian' Belgians, the Dutch businessman is determined, ambitious, "a real fox". In supplier/customer situations it is often a question of "all or nothing" - the relationship is either a roaring success or it goes straight off the rails.

Belgian businesspeople find the Dutch can be less than wholehearted in their respect for the letter, let alone the spirit, of the agreements they sign. The problem, they claim, can be either deviousness or plain bad faith. At the same time, they give them the highest marks of all the European business communities for creativity. There may not be a contradiction here.

An example of this creativity is offered by the true-story case of the Dutch boss of a manufacturing company who was dissatisfied with the performance of the head of his French marketing subsidiary. Without warning the latter, he decided to advertise for a replacement in the French newspress. He then decided that the incumbent was OK after all, so he allocated the advertisement costs to the wretched Frenchman's operating budget...

One head better than two?

Dutch management philosophy is evolving fast - and in some ways moving counter to current trends. The traditional collective approach, reflecting the Dutch democratic instinct that teamwork is preferable to individual initiative, is now being progressively supplanted by *eenkoppig management* ('single-headed management'). People are, sometimes reluctantly, starting to accept the role of the entrepreneur and to reward entrepreneurial behaviour.

114

This evolution owes a lot to the development of an excellent management educational curriculum by Rotterdam's Erasmus University. Other significant initiatives in the business field include Nijenrode University (originally known as NOIB) and, more recently, NIMBAS in Utrecht. The country shows less allegiance to the engineering tradition than Germany though, dubiously for a democratic country, applies class distinctions in this discipline between the university-trained engineers (civil engineer, Ir) and his technical high school-trained equivalent (technical engineer, Ing).

Some foreign observers also say the Dutch are becoming more creative. They are moving into new areas of business and technology faster than the Germans: while the latter prefer to tinker with existing systems, the Dutch know they have to develop entirely new ones.

The relationship between business and government is also a suitably pragmatic one. There is little of the government-led intervention so favoured by the French, and the links between the different estates are less formalised than Germany. Philips, which used to be government-led, is now emphatically market-minded.

Yet it is hardly surprising that, in a relatively tight little country, there should be a lot of mutual sympathy between governors and governed: years ago a journalist by the name of Mertens drew up a list of 200 families who, he believed, controlled the economy of The Netherlands. This mutual sympathy, however, finds expression discreetly and to outward appearances democratically.

Perhaps surprisingly for a free trade-minded country, mutual sympathy also applies between local companies and local suppliers - a normal phenomenon in many other parts of Europe. A Belgian production director observes that the Dutch are almost as chauvinistic in their buying habits as the Germans. The Scots engineering director of a major US multinational complains that "the Dutch will use every possible device to keep business within the family. They cheat. The solution I adopted was to send in a Greek. He knows how to beat them at their own game!"

In contrast, a Belgian brought in to run the Dutch subsidiary of an American multinational (a challenge if there ever was one) first noted the tendency to close office doors, rather like the Germans, but later came to acknowledge the relative readiness - compared with their neighbours, the Belgians and Germans, or even the French - to accept the advice and experience of outsiders. Despite their reputation for dogmatism, the Dutch are much more open to third-party opinion than their Belgian neighbours and are not too frugal to pay for it. So much for the stereotypes!

No examination of the Dutch business culture would be complete without reference to the skills of a certain class of Dutchman - generally the self-employed type - in turning events to his advantage and to the detriment of the other party. This character contrasts starkly with the stereotype of the tough-dealing, matter-of-fact and ultimately decent Dutchman, some of whom will even spurn a written agreement and be happy with a handshake.

That the two cohabit in a single culture may be due to the fact that, as a very seasoned Dutchman pointed out to me: "History has created two types of Dutchmen, the farmers and the pirates. You're talking of the pirates."

An American businessman I know has had the misfortune to be involved in a series of disastrous multilateral deals. To use his own words: "There was always a Dutchman at the middle of them."

Happily not everyone shares this experience. A Swedish international marketing director comments: "All my Swedish friends say 'watch it!' when you start working with the Dutch. But The Netherlands is one of the easiest countries in which to do business. As far as I'm concerned, they are correct, there's no double-dealing, and they pay on time."

A cautious attitude to life can indeed spur the search for artful solutions. Under pressure the Dutch, who are generally a very correct people, may conjure up stratagems which do credit to their ingenuity but not necessarily to their sense of honour. Curiously, many of them are also great natural gamblers, a quality they sometimes put to use in business.

At least, as a senior Belgian woman executive says: "The Dutch can be tricky, but they have the candour to admit it"...

"It's difficult to do business with them. It's not that the game plan changes, it's that they move to a new playing field"

American multinational executive

"The Belgian solution is based on compromise"

John Mole, *Mind your Manners*

"We lack rigueur. We're not analytical enough, we don't have the mental disciplines"

Belgian marketing director

"'Belgianisation' - the abandonment of national responsibilities in favour of totally commercial values"

Leon Trotsky

"The Belgian defers to any authority, yet in his heart he is a convinced anarchist"

German expatriate journalist

"I have found no other case in the world of two neighbouring countries having so much in common and still showing such differences in their mental programming"

Geert Hofstede,
speaking about the Netherlands and Belgium

"Belgians don't have a blush factor"

British journalist

"When we're in trouble, we talk. When the Walloons talk, they're in trouble"

Flemish joke

"Walloons resent being regarded as quaint Frenchmen"

John Mole, *Mind your Manners*

"I need mediocre people"

Ageing Walloon entrepreneur

BELGIUM

W hen a Belgian says 'buy a Frenchman for what he's worth and sell him for what he thinks he's worth', the joke tells you as much about the Belgians as about the French.

The Belgians are salespeople by instinct and, if anything, manufacturers by accident (the presence of extensive coal deposits sparked a mini-industrial revolution in the early 19th century). They may not be as skilful traders as the Dutch, but the latter increasingly confine these skills to a segment of their society whereas, in Belgium, the selling mentality seems to be endemic.

If not actually sales representatives, the Belgians are merchants, wholesalers, distributors, retailers and, above all, exporters. I have even met Belgian export salesmen flogging reproduction Persian carpets to the design-conscious Danes, a feat that almost surpasses the traditional sale of iceboxes to eskimos. I know of another carpet manufacturer who hit on the idea of selling 'offcuts', individually equipped with compasses to facilitate alignment with Mecca, as personalised prayermats for fervent muslims, of which there are many. No wonder Belgium returns a higher per capita export sales figure than any other country in the world...

One wonders where they find all the stuff to export. Having even sold off their industrial heritage to foreign interests, particularly the French, Belgium looks increasingly like a satellite economy. And an important contribution to this export performance comes from the local production of foreign multinationals, mainly American. But this cannot explain it on its own. While the country has some excellent big companies - names like Bekaert, Petrofina, Solvay and UCB - the answer lies largely in the productivity and dynamism of Belgium's SME sector.

There is a major concentration of middle-size and relatively mature SMEs, particularly in the Flemish half of the country. As the people who come highest, of all western Europeans, on Hofstede's uncertainty avoidance dimension, it is perhaps surprising that the Belgians should show this degree of entrepreneurialism.

A study undertaken in 1993 by Rotterdam's Erasmus University concluded that Belgian entrepreneurs as a whole

121

dislike risktaking and cultivate compromise "with conservatism" (they are also found to put the need to find a solution before the logic of the arguments involved which, the Dutch researchers concede, can encourage "creative results"). In fact, as an American consultant points out, the Walloons seem to be more natural risktakers than the Flemish, as evidenced by the number of entrepreneurs indulging in what look like rather risky grassroots ventures.

As if the evidence weren't there, Hofstede and other researchers confirm quite emphatically the differences between the Belgians and the Dutch. It is as if the frontiers of the Roman Empire were still intact. But this long-past historical fact fails to explain fully the difference between the emphatic and often outspoken attitudes of the Dutch and the nuanced and sometimes evasive behaviour of the Flemish.

There are other historical factors which, in the opinions of some, are equally important. The Dutch have been heard to say that anyone who could stomach the Spanish Inquisition would be capable of anything. A Flemish friend puts it in more reasonable terms, evoking the 'braindrains' that occurred when the educated and relatively liberal classes of Flanders fled northwards from the armies of the Duke of Alba in the late-1500s and, more recently, when Belgium won its independence from the Netherlands in 1830.

The ability to make the best of a bad thing is also evident in the story recounted to me by the Belgian ex-inmate of a German prisoner-of-war camp in WWII. There were 3,500 prisoners, of whom about 3,000 were French, 350 Belgian, 100 British and the remaining 50 of various nationalities. Within a few weeks of confinement, this social microcosm had generated its own section leaders and barrack-room heads, as in any prison camp at the time. Yet of the 142 more or less self-appointed bosses who emerged in this case, 115 of them were Belgian.

My informant, who was one of the Belgian prisoners, attributed this partly to the truculence of the French, but more importantly to a Belgian sense of *débrouillardise* (a French word but one that Belgians, Flemish as much as Walloons, really understand the meaning of). To this should be added the national desire to eat well and, not altogether

122

incidentally, the fact that many of the Belgians, being Flemish, spoke passable German.

Opportunists and anarchists

The Belgians also owe it to unwanted visitors - Spanish, Austrian, French, Dutch, German, the list is almost endless - that, as a result, they developed a very strong attachment to their environment, a remarkable sense of community identity. This rather unbusinesslike quality inevitably interferes with people's mobility. Yet most educated Belgians, particularly the Flemish, are admirably open-minded and cosmopolitan people, except in regard to their internal squabbles.

History seemingly has taught the Belgians to make the best of a bad job. They have learned to be opportunists, a quality that serves them well - and, on occasion, badly. They manage to tolerate barmy bureaucracy, of which there is a lot, while at heart they are anarchists. Maybe they are encouraged by Geert Hofstede's assertion that "even ineffective rules satisfy people's emotional need for formal structure" - and, as strong uncertainty avoidance people, the Belgians certainly need structure.

Hofstede also noted the enormous differences in value systems and mentality between the Dutch and the Belgians. It is as if the Romans knew exactly what they were doing when they drew up the frontiers of their empire, though the Burgundians probably had more to do with the final result. Moreover the Hermes project and other studies also confirmed the underlying similarities in thinking between the two communities, Flemish and Walloon.

An Australian CEO, who headed up the Belgian manufacturing subsidiary of a US multinational for many years, remarked that the Belgians "want to be good friends with everyone. They are comfortable with compromise, in fact they don't like black-and-white situations. Rather than make the big decisions, they would prefer somebody else played the boss."

This phenomenon explains an oft-repeated observation made to me by foreign CEOs of a number of Benelux operations (culturally, a Benelux cluster is a nonsense!). When proposing a course of action to a Dutch team, there would be extensive discussion, even disagreement. Putting the same proposal to a Belgian team, there would be little discussion... but the team members would then go away and tear the idea to bits. There is a strong strain of passivity, almost fatalism, in the mind of many Belgians.

The Swedish director of the Dutch and Belgian subsidiaries of a business machines company confirms that on the big issues the Dutch are prepared to argue over matters of principle, whereas the Belgians tend to go along with what management says, even if they don't agree (the problems come later). Yet, on the smaller issues like buying a photocopier, the Dutch will buy a machine straight from the catalogue while the Belgians will ask for a demonstration model and try it out first. Where the Dutch are defiant, the Belgians are simply mistrustful. There's a world of difference between neighbours.

When it comes to paying for things, the Belgians can be just as difficult as the Dutch. But again there is a difference: where the Dutch will examine an offer in detail, dourly and realistically, the Belgians will look at the outward appearance of things and often delve no further. In the words of a British consultant, "they have a bargain mentality". The discount is sometimes more important to them than the net price.

The mistrustful nature of the Belgians is also evident in the reluctance of companies to employ consultants. Most Belgians, Flemish and Walloon, seem to think they know everything there is to know and don't need help from anyone, thank you - particularly when it costs real money. But there are some differences between the two communities in business. A Brussels headhunter reports that when he calls 'sources' for leads on potential candidates, the Flemish always cooperate openly whereas the French speakers, Brussels or Walloon, are decidedly reticent. Walloon businesses also tend to be more autocratic and hierarchical than their Flemish counterparts.

The 'downside' of Belgian opportunism is a lack of consistency on matters strategic. Belgian managers do not find it that easy to think long-term, and they find it even more difficult to stay with a long-term decision. I have had the

I offer the following story, recounted to me by a man on a train, as an example of Belgian export entrepreneurialism.

My informant imported beachwear, primarily for sale in Belgium. Due to strikes and stoppages, his Italian manufacturer was nine months late with that year's fashions. Our Belgian felt obligated to accept the product, despite the fact that the summer season was over, for the sake of good future relations with his supplier. But where could he sell a few thousand items of beachwear in late-Autumn?

After due reflection, and although he had never seriously tackled the market before, he thought Miami might be worth a try, particularly since he knew someone in the trade there who, despite limited resources, had good local contacts. So our man took an Air Bahamas flight at less than half the scheduled rate and, with his friend, combed the waterfront shops from one end of Miami Beach to the other. He had disposed of all his merchandise even before he had got three-quarters of the way along, selling at half the average price for Belgium and accepting payment direct. He also persuaded his customers to guarantee reimbursement of a sum equivalent to the US import duty if this was waived retrospectively - which it was. So he cleared his stocks, covered his costs, eventually made a modest profit on the deal, and kept his supplier happy. He also opened a new market!

experience of seeing a marketing strategy which had been elaborated at some expense, and involved a considerable investment in equipment, abandoned within two months - long before any judgement could be made on its effectiveness. The mental stamina isn't there.

Commodity products, niche markets

As in France, the aristocrat of Belgian industry has traditionally been the engineer. This is partly the French influence, partly the fact that, in the course of their mini-industrial revolution, the Belgians learned skills downstream from their coal and steel industries: in metallurgy, metalworking and machine production. The result, among other things, was the emergence of the Société Générale de Belgique, a conglomerate holding active in all these sectors and others, and reputed post-WWII to control no less than 60 per cent of the Belgian economy. The 'old lady', courted by Carlo de Benedetti, threw herself into the arms of the French.

The reliance on these traditional industries was reinforced by circumstances which distracted from the need to develop other skills. First, until 1960, the substantial flows of income from the country's African interests encouraged a false sense of security. The country was also in the fortunate position of emerging from WWII with a reasonably intact industrial base which, in the undiscriminating mood of the times, was able to meet a sizeable segment of European demand. Finally Belgium was, and still is, a relatively open market - and this worked as much to the country's favour as against it.

Also, as David Granick pointed out as long ago as 1962, "because Belgium itself has followed a low-tariff policy, Belgian companies do not find it profitable to produce 'growth products' even for the small Belgian market; their factories could not achieve the same economies of large-scale production as their competitors from larger nations."

The result is that Belgium has either tended, in the case of its less inventive entrepreneurs, to skim off business by an opportunistic policy of marginal pricing, or has more intelligently sought refuge in niche markets. There are also some areas of commodity production where Belgian entrepreneurs, through persistant penetration of European markets, have succeeded in achieving economies of scale despite the modest size of the country's economy - and this long before the Single Market was ever thought of. Moreover the ' Best of Belgium ' is extremely good : quality is second nature to Belgians, and something they share with others.

All of which says a lot for the sheer guts and 'get-up-and-go' of many Belgian entrepreneurs. Yet, on balance, it is questionable whether the country has learned from its experience. Belgian businesspeople still tend to think too much in simple supply-demand terms, with the emphasis on the price they can get for their products, and not enough on such sophisticated issues as marketing, positioning and product enhancement.

A study undertaken by the PA Consulting Group in 1989 showed that Belgian manufacturers still focus too little on what products they make and too much on the process by which they make them. We are back to the engineer - whose status (*burgerlijk ingenieur/ingénieur civil*) is as fiercely protected in Belgium as it is in The Netherlands.

But Belgian universities are responding rapidly to the new realities, producing some of the best young talent in such esoteric areas as bio-engineering, microelectronics, artificial intelligence, and more mundane things like marketing and product positioning. Belgian business schools provide sound training, though still rather lacking in creativity, alongside local implantations of US business schools and some new creations that are jumping onto the European bandwagon. Their standards are variable: one of the latter awards a degree which is sufficient to get its graduates automatically eliminated from a multinational's list of candidates...

Despite their hangups Belgians, besides being good and conscientious workers, are realists - the dictates of international business are telling them that they need to clean up their act. It remains to be seen whether it is not too late. If it is, then the best Belgian managers will gravitate - as they are already doing - to the world of the multinationals where, thanks to their essentially openminded, pragmatic and uncomplicated attitudes, they will prosper.

The 'Think Global, Act Local' slogan, which works well for many companies, has its limits. One of these, bordering on insanity, is 'Think Global, Act Benelux', a mental package which does credit to the pre-WWII customs union but shows no respect for cultural realities. Belgium and the Netherlands (those bits north of Limburg and North Brabant provinces) are like chalk and cheese.

Geert Hofstede says that he has never come across two neighbouring countries and cultures so different from one another as The Netherlands and Belgium. As both an eminent social psychologist and a Dutchman, he knows what he's talking about.

The Scottish chief engineer of one of the world's automotive giants discovered this for himself when he commissioned a Flemish Belgian civil engineering consultancy to supervise construction of a plant extension for a new production line. The consultancy hired a team of technicians specifically for the project. Some of them were Flemish, the others Dutch.

A few weeks into the construction phase, up to which point everything had been running smoothly, our Scottish friend learned that the specifications for the new car model would require an additional finishing stage and that this would require x square meters of extra space. He called in the Flemish project manager and agreed with him on the changes: an end-wall moved y meters further out and six pillars repositioned.

The project manager, being Flemish and culturally attuned to change and compromise, had no problem with this. Nor did his Flemish technicians, who cheerfully did what they were told and never asked questions. But the Dutch technicians, when they heard of the changes, first wanted to know why and agonised over the situation, then had the greatest difficulty in retraining their mental sights on the new objective (once they did, they worked as well as the Flemish).

The project was completed satisfactorily and on schedule, though not on budget. The Scottish chief engineer then called the Flemish project manager into his office and said: "We're certainly going to have another job like this before long and we'll certainly consider your company for the project. But on one condition: no Dutchmen on the team...!"

"I have never met a people so prone to self-criticism, and yet so nationalistic as the Swedes"

Jean Phillips-Martinsson, *Swedes as Others see Them*

"Strange bods, the Swedes. Been dealing with them for years but they never keep in touch once a sale has been made"

British sales executive

"It is very difficult to make conversation with a Swede"

French businessman

"If a Norwegian is badly treated in Denmark, it is because the Dane thinks he is a Swede - not all Danes can tell the difference"

Danish businessman

"Norwegians often appear to be 'village folk' as opposed to 'city folk'. In the main they don't have the self-confidence of, say, the Danes"

British business executive

"Norwegians are outspoken to the degree of being naive... The Swedes are honest to a less degree, the Danes not at all"

Finnish businessman

"In Denmark, breaking rules and laws is one of our most popular pastimes"

Danish businessman

"Finns are rotten writers. We prefer the telephone to the letter, a telex is normally the nearest thing to a written confirmation"

Finnish businessman

"It is commonly known that one of the worst things for a Norwegian is to be taken in by a Dane"

Danish sales executive

130

SWEDEN

(and neighbours)

The Swedes are very self-focussed", says a Dane with just a little bit of feeling. "They have a highly developed culture and they think highly of it. This tends to make them hypercritical towards other cultures. If you find someone complaining about the bill in an international business hotel, as likely as not it's a Swede..."

To most other Europeans the Swedes come across as professional and sophisticated businesspeople. They even have a reputation for second-guessing, which sometimes raises questions about their intentions. But generally they are pleasant people to deal with and courteous in a rather old-fashioned way. Their 'psycho-poles'? Permissiveness and conservatism.

The Swedes dominate in the Nordic arena by the strength of their traditional industries built around the Wallenberg empire, spawning a family of originally rather colonialist but ultimately very successful multinationals that today account for some 40 per cent of the Swedish stockmarket (as *The Economist* says, "a concentration of economic power unequalled in Europe", at least since the undoing of Belgium's Société Générale). Swedish big business has had to be outward-looking. In fact the 'Top 20' Nordic firms do 80 per cent of their business abroad. Most of them are Swedish.

Despite its socialist trappings, Sweden is an essentially capitalist country with much of the national wealth concentrated in the private sector, though the massive concentrations of power - in what in some cases are still essentially family holdings - are dissipating with changes in the laws on voting rights. It is in many respects a very mature industry - compared with its Nordic neighbours who are busy demonstrating that there is almost as much entrepreneurialism in each of their more youthful economies as you will now find in Sweden.

In fact the Swedes have a certain reluctance to be unduly entrepreneurial. It may seem slightly surprising (see box page 136) that it should be a German businesswoman, i.e. someone from a relatively strong uncertainty avoidance culture, who comments that Swedish managers prefer to stick to proven methods rather than take chances. But management academics make the same point. The explanation is that, while the Swedes have the second lowest uncertainty avoidance rating in Europe next to the Danes, they do believe in **risk** avoidance - and, as I explained in Chapter 2, this is not the same thing.

Jean Phillips-Martinsson speaks in her book *Swedes as Others see Them*[30] about "the lack of a spirit of adventure, the fear to take risks, over-cautiousness and delay in taking decisions and meeting delivery deadlines...". Matters are not helped by the transition, still not complete, from an autocratic to a participative and decentralised style of management.

Ms Phillips-Martinsson speaks of an opinion poll she conducted among 171 foreign businessmen to discover how the Swedish businessman is rated in the world. "In brief", she concludes, "the Swedish businessman was regarded as inflexible in his negotiations and behaviour - unwilling to discuss and adjust, slow to make decisions, avoids conflict, over-cautious, and a stickler for punctuality. Difficult to get to know, hard to work with and for, stiff, no fun, dull and conceited."! Anyone disagree?

An American multinational executive speaks of the Swedes as "difficult to deal with, you have to find common ground and then keep the fire going. They used to have a habit of saying 'we don't do it that way in Sweden', and still seem to be fearful of foreign ideas and influences. But from time to time they can come up with some very radical blue-sky ideas, some of which work very well. At other times they just get carried away and ignore the underlying realities."

Many people comment on the shyness of the average Swede, often dissimulated behind a facade of courteousness but occasionally, when under stress, manifesting itself in an excessive self-assertiveness. Jean Phillips-Martinsson cites the words of a Frenchman she interviewed: "There is a kind of shyness in a way, and aggressiveness in others, a kind of superiority complex in some cases, and inferiority complex in others."

Some words on their neighbours

In business, the Nordic countries have the youngest managers in Europe and run their businesses very democratically,

134

as young managers should. Geert Hofstede classes the Nordics as 'feminine' in the sense that they genuinely believe in social equality, put personal relationships before money and have a high regard for the quality of life.

Management practices quite understandably tend to reflect the egalitarian culture and social organisation of the Nordic countries. Conscious of the need to compete in international markets from a relatively remote location, management education is receiving increasing attention from institutions like Uppsala University, the Swedish Institute of Management (IFL) and the Jönköping International Business School in Sweden; the Copenhagen Business High School and the Nils Brock institutes in Denmark; the Norwegian School of Management outside Oslo and the Norwegian School of Economics and Business Administration in Bergen; and the Helsinki School of Economics and Tampere University's School of Business Administration in Finland.

Though many of us find the Nordics confusingly alike - and Geert Hofstede's research shows up some of the similarities - there are still differences in the mentality and business cultures of the Swedes and their neighbours, the Danes, the Norwegians and the Finns.

Moreover Sweden is losing its dubious advantage as a nation that industrialised relatively early. Instead of the Swedish model, people now talk about the Danish model and cite entrepreneurial examples like ISS, Danfoss, Novo Nordisk, Rockwool, Bruel & Kjaer, Grundfos and of course Lego. The Danes have developed into consummate marketers, while the Norwegians are more traders by nature.

The *Wall Street Journal Europe*, referring to Denmark's ability to survive in an international environment, even called the country "the Tomorrowland of the European Community".

And yet, many of the businesspeople I have talked to end up scratching their heads when we get to the subject of 'the Danes'. The word that comes up most often in conversation on this topic is "relaxed". Listen to the words of this British senior executive who ran the Nordic and Benelux operations of a major service multinational: "I found the Danes the most frustrating people to manage. It was very difficult to

135

get them to realise the need to work hard. They're terribly relaxed, too easygoing." He added that they could be both dogmatic and unrealistic in one and the same breath.

Another multinational executive, who happens to be a Dane, cautions that this laid-back attitude should not be interpreted as a lack of energy or motivation. "You have to understand that the Danish way of life places more emphasis on leisure time than some other European cultures. Even more important, the state doesn't give you the encouragement to work longer hours or harder: the impact of the current taxation system is such that there is no personal financial incentive. It is impossible for a company executive to get rich in Denmark, unlike some other European countries. By the time you've paid your taxes, the differentials between one management grade and the next are marginal." This of course also applies in varying degrees to the other Nordic societies.

Yet the entrepreneurial spirit is highly developed in the Danes: many executives voluntarily terminate a successful corporate career to go into business on their own account. If they do manage to amass a bit of money in addition to experience, there's a fair chance they will go independent.

John Mole speaks of "a deep commitment to autonomy and independence", both at the national and at the personal level. A Finnish businessman rates the Danes as "the most assertive and apparently self-assured of the Nordic peoples". He says "apparently" because you can never be sure where you are with the Nordics...

As for the Norwegians, our Danish informant mentioned earlier finds them more relaxed than the Swedes - and even more than his own people. "It's easy to talk with the Norwegians and get things done." He agrees, however, that they also can be very stubborn and dogmatic.

Norwegians Kjell Habert and Arild Lillebø sampled 110 foreign businessmen who deal regularly with their compatriots and summed up a collective verdict on the Norwegian business community in their book *Made in Norway*: "They appear inappropriately dressed, seem to have problems with holding their liquor, not to be punctual, slow to make contact with foreigners, indifferent to liberal arts issues, unaware of their English language limitations, poor communicators, conflict-avoiding, naive and unsophisticated; they often make false business assumptions and are both cautious and impatient as negotiators." Gulp! It is only fair to add that many of these characteristics are shared by their neighbours.

It would be wrong to conclude that Norwegian business is crammed with unsophisticates. There are a few impressive corporations like Statoil, Norsk Hydro, Kvaerner and Tiedemann, and a bevy of clever little 'niche' companies engaged in the manufacture of things like bran biscuits, handcreams and fish-hooks. Unfortunately it happens all too often that, in the words of a German businessman interviewed by Habert and Lillebø, "the Norwegians produce first and start marketing afterwards - with the work preferably carried out by a sales engineer rather than by a marketing man."

The odd ones out

The Finns also qualify as being relaxed, though in a rather impenetrable way, locked as they are into their physical and cultural environment, with a formidable educational system which teaches them, among other things, not to say anything until they're sure it makes absolute sense. Communication does not come easy.

Perhaps because of this, and as many observers have commented, the Finns can at times be unexpectedly emotional: "I have actually had customers crying in front of me for sympathy, because of their worries about the future of their business." This is confirmed by a British business journalist who says it is not uncommon to have a well lubricated professional lunchtime *tête-à-tête* terminate with soulbaring and tearful revelations of marital infidelity, deaths in the family and so on.

Finnish business, like Swedish business, still shows some signs of the German influence. It is said to go back to pioneering companies like Enso-Gutzeit (note the German origins!), big vertically integrated bureaucracies which created a taste for hierarchy. Professor Kakabadse and associates[31] also speak of the "concentration of boardroom power in Finnish industry" and of a tradition of employee loyalty reflected in "a high degree of job mobility within a single organisation."

Today's conditions are eroding these traditions of Finnish industry: the participative approach is extending from other areas of Finnish society into business. The Finns, perhaps because of the cultural and linguistic barriers they have to cross to do business with the rest of the world, are very careful once they have made the transition. A British consultant comments on the human resources skills of Kone, a medium size Finnish multinational: "They were very impressive in the sensitive way they inducted an Italian acquisition into their culture."

A successful Finnish executive who works for a multinational says that "the Finns can indeed live with structure and

138

discipline, but hierarchy is another matter. Finnish industry may have been hierarchical, but it is changing fast."

But, as Professor Kakabadse states, "if anyone adopts too individualistic a style, then he or she is likely to have an adverse impact on the generation of and commitment to implementing strategies for the future." And, further on: "Development in entrepreneurial skills and ways of working may be an important need for Finnish managers working for multinationals in fast-evolving market conditions."

The Cranfield study concludes that the capacity of Finnish executives "to manage difficulties, sensitivities and different contingencies is high." Such human qualities extend, as one might expect of countries with a tradition of consensus, to Finland's Nordic neighbours: "there is a greater preponderance of effective communication and delegation and higher levels of managerial maturity among Finnish and Swedish top managers than among most others in Europe."

But, in the opinion of those involved, Nordic business aptitudes still vary dramatically. If one is to believe the old Norwegian saw (it somehow seems right that 'old saws' should be Norwegian), it should be the Finns who design the products, the Swedes who make them, the Danes who sell them... and the Norwegians, because they think anything foreign is better than the home-grown equivalent, who buy them. But since the Lillehammer Winter Olympics the Norwegians have decided that, on second thoughts, Norwegian is best.

No chapter on the Nordics would be complete without reference to the role of silence (I leave the Danes out of this). Its significance is best summed up in a story I heard from a French professor at Vaasa University who has been studying Finnish-French business relationships. It concerns the top (and significantly English-speaking) salesman of a French equipment company who was invited to make a product presentation to the board of a Finnish corporation. When he completed what was an excellent half-hour presentation, he ran into a wall of silence: the Finns were reflecting and thinking what to say next (they had already agreed amongst themselves in principle to buy the product). But the Frenchman, in acute discomfort at the lack of feedback, panicked and decided to repeat what he had said. A half-hour later he had lost the contract!

"Danish punctuality would result in hypertension in Greece"

Max Messmer, *Staffing Europe*

"... the British have formalised unpunctuality so that it is impolite to be on time"

John Mole, *Mind your Manners*

"The Poles, amongst others, complained that the Swedes were always in a hurry to return home, especially on a Friday, instead of staying the weekend to complete the business"

Jean-Phillips Martinsson, *Swedes as Others see Them*

"Skipping lunch is virtually unheard of"

Helen Wattley Ames, *Spain is Different*

"Portuguese steel mill employee Carlos Boja has been fired because he turned up early for work five days in a row. The mill's owner Jose Aruajo disliked Boja's over-punctuality, and told of how 'I appreciate him being early for work but when he ignored my orders [to come at the usual time] I had to fire him'"

Europa Times, October 1993

"For all their egalitarian claims, the French seem to cherish pecking orders and the perks that go with them"

Barsoux and Lawrence, *Management in France*

"The boss is on holiday and no decisions are taken in his absence"

Belgian executive secretary

"The often strongly emotional character of hierarchical relationships in France is intriguing. There is an extreme diversity of feelings towards superiors: they may be either adored or despised with equal intensity. This situation is not at all universal: we found it neither in the Netherlands nor in the USA"

Philippe d'Iribarne[32] (quoted by Geert Hofstede)

"Germans sense their own space as an extension of the ego"

Edward T Hall, *The Hidden Dimension*

Chapter 4

The Nerve Ends

of punctuality
and pecking orders

It almost goes without saying that, by the European norm (if such a thing exists!), the most eccentric time-related behaviour occurs at the extremes, south **and** north.

One of the curious things for a northerner is to discover that some southerners, the Spanish in particular, tend to turn punctuality inside out and use arriving late as a way of emphasising superiority. Unpunctuality is, in their book, a status symbol.

Even in structured situations, the Spanish are still known to adopt the *mañana* approach. Richard Mead cites the case of a university lecturer who habitually put in an appearance 20 minutes late: once his students had taken due note of the fact, they also arrived 20 minutes late. The same can be said of the French with their 'diplomatic quarter' and even the Swedes with **their** 'academic quarter'. The optional quarter hour, whether dubbed academic or diplomatic, is said to owe its inspiration to a **Swedish** professor who left home for his midday lecture when the university clock struck twelve. He had a 15-minute walk in front of him and his students soon got wise...

So not too much should be made of this *mañana* thing. Provided everyone synchronises, it comes to the same whether one arrives on time or not - the only ones put out are the foreigners.

But it does have to be said that the Spanish **do** have a rather casual attitude towards time - not a *mañana* mentality, but an erratic appreciation where something that has been hanging fire for years becomes the burning issue of the moment. This can also result in the belief that, in the words of John Mole, "delivery dates are often approximations not to be taken literally."

Many foreigners entertain the idea that the *mañana* approach colours every aspect of Spanish life. This is not the case. Spaniards can have every bit as great a sense of urgency as anyone else. But, then, there are important but understandable differences in interpretation between the Andalusians, for example, and the people further north in the Iberian peninsula. As Helen Wattley Ames says, "the further north one goes, the more intense the work ethic becomes. The Basques and Catalans are famous in Spain for their industriousness and acquisitive instinct..."

Climate obviously plays a part: the *mañana* mentality is particularly evident in southern Spain, the Mezzogiorno of Italy, even in Portugal. The lack of a sense of urgency can also take the form of simple insouciance, like the Italian manager who kept on accepting impossible deadlines from his Anglo-Saxon head office despite the fact that he knew full well (and they did too) that he couldn't honour them. But again, like the Spanish university students and their professor, you all know where you are after a while.

The compensation for lack of punctuality is that, if your host is Latin, he or she will probably make up for it by giving you more time than you actually expected (which means of course that the next appointment will be even later still). Or the following may happen, as John Mole points out, if you arrive on time in Italy: "You are equally likely to be invited in to the tail end of a host's previous appointment as to be kept waiting outside. If the ensuing conversation is promising the two meetings may be rolled into one, someone else steps in and you all end up going out to lunch together." Very disarming but only possible because, in Dr Hall's words, Italians are polychronic people.

One of the results of this is that Italians, like other Mediterraneans, have an aversion to making arrangements well in advance. The more impromptu the occasion, the more likely it is to actually happen!

As for the rest of Europe, strange things can happen there too. Understandably the best timekeepers are the German Swiss (they are even known to turn up early), with the Finns in hard pursuit. After them come the Germans, the Danes and the Swedes (although the last-named say that, if summoned to a meeting at 2 pm, they arrive after the first stroke of the clock and before the second). The Swedes are also notorious for setting a one-hour time limit to meetings - after 60 minutes, they blow the whistle.

The Norwegians by comparison are somewhat unNordic in their attitude to time, evoking the 'academic quarter hour', similar to the French businessperson's 'diplomatic quarter hour'. Even the British nowadays tend to turn up more or less on time, except on social occasions when it's good taste to arrive 15-20 minutes late. But the Dutch (maybe because they are late from the last, overcharged meeting) have a reputation with others for arriving late for business appointments, and don't seem to be particularly bothered about it.

As the day is long...

Describing the typical business and social timetables of the different European cultures would fill a book in its own right: in any case such books exist for every country. Suffice it to say here that, as you move through Europe from north to south, things tend to happen later - and 'bubbles of space' (see page 20) get smaller .

At a particular latitude climate again takes over. In Italy, north of Rome, the typical workday is 9 am-6 pm, the habitual lunchhour 1-2 pm and dinner 8 pm. From Rome southwards workdays are shorter, lunch is at 2-3 pm and dinner at 9 pm.

A typical Spanish workday in July-August will be 8 am-3 pm latest, when the heat becomes intolerable, but in these six or seven hours a lot of work will be done. Lunch is at 3 pm

---

Time is Money...

Anyone who works to the precept that 'time is money' is in for some surprises. The only sense in which this can be said to be universally true for Europe is in reluctance to pay bills promptly.

Even here, there are significant differences. According to Intrum Justitia, **contractual** payment terms in Italy (66 days) and France (60 days) are twice what they are in The Netherlands (28 days) and the UK (29 days). The latter get their own back, though, by taking relatively long to pay (51 and 53 days respectively).

A spokesman for Dun & Bradstreet, the business information supplier, summed it up with the words: "With such a varied picture of payment habits in Europe, it has to be stressed that companies trading across borders need to be particularly vigilant before deciding credit terms." Amen.

---

and, in the summer, life only really starts after 10 pm, probably 11.30 in the summer months.

In most continental countries, business breakfasts are still decidedly unpopular - and particularly so with the French who these days, at least in Paris, rarely seem to get up in time. A Belgian executive says that the managers in his company's French subsidiary "rarely get into the office before 10 am to avoid the traffic, then go for a long lunch which can last until 3 pm. They finally come back and actually do some work until about 6 and then hang around until 7-7.30 to avoid the traffic - and without necessarily doing any work!" The whole country downs tools in August.

Normal office hours in Sweden, flexitime permitting, are 8 am to 4.30 pm. The Swedes and most Nordics take a month off in the summer like the French, but in their case it's July.

The Norwegians also get to work at 8 am, take their lunch at 11 am and **walk** home to be in time for dinner at 5 pm: from that time on until the next morning, most towns look as if they have been neutroned.

A British multinational executive commented that the Norwegians "will give you **four** good days of work - as long as they can be sure of getting away at the weekend to their cabin by the fjord."

He went on to say that he found his Danish employees insensitive to urgency, particularly when it encroached on their private time. "We finish at five, and that's that!". In fact the safest thing is to assume that, for any of the Nordic countries, the working day ends at 4 pm and the week at midday Friday.

Prompted by the official and largely misguided strategy of getting people to spend less time at work so as to create employment for more people, German executives seem to be working less and less. The British meanwhile are earning a new reputation as the workaholics of Europe.

As for the European business year as a whole, this seems to be getting progressively shorter. Possibly as a reflection of the stress imposed by downsizing, executives of all countries are spending longer periods away from the office. In a multinational and multicultural country like Belgium, it is getting difficult these days to do anything between the beginning of December and the end of January. In fact it is not very easy to do anything the rest of the year, when most corporate executives seem to spend all their time in conference rooms, hotels and airplanes.

The Status Game

In low power distance countries like Sweden, to come back to Hofstede's dimension, hierarchy plays a minor role. Even in high power distance countries like France - where it assumes symbolic, even heraldic, proportions - it is acceptable, even to those disfavoured hierarchically, precisely because they know the system.

Consider the dilemma of the poor foreign sales executive visiting France, who has the option of either talking to the top management of a company - without realising that the real decision-making capability lies further down the line with someone of whom both he and they are largely unaware - or of talking to someone further down the line in the hope that no one further up will notice. Either way, if his strategem fails, his efforts will be wasted...

Of course, the issue of hierarchy can get in the way of sensible management in any country. But some European cultures, particularly the Nordic ones, reduce this to a non-issue by instinctively favouring the concept of the flatter organisation, with teamwork and consensus decision-making.

Other cultures, the Mediterranean ones, exclude such issues by firmly investing all responsibility in one person, the boss. It is the cultures in between, like France and to a lesser extent Germany and the United Kingdom, that are left with the problem of reconciling hierarchy with the urgent need to improve efficiency internally and enhance transparency with the world outside.

Hierarchy of course has its status symbols which, again, vary from one culture to another. Let's start with a particularly hierarchical society, the French.

As Richard Mead says, many French companies were modelled on the family business and priority was given to being close to the workforce. This led to the tradition amongst French managers, even corporate executives, of occupying a central office which bestowed symbolic value on the occupant. The thought that this was also a vantage point from which to supervise the activities of those less fortunate than the boss was not alien to the idea.

This arrangement is still common in private business, both in France and Belgium. I know a Flemish owner-manager who occupies an office immediately opposite the main and only entrance/exit to his manufacturing and marketing establishment (which incidentally employs over 500 people) so that he can personally police late arrivers and early leavers.

In the bigger French companies, according to Barsoux and Lawrence, senior executives can be as exercised by the principle of their subordinates not being able to look in as by their own ability to look out: "The French like to have a 'territory' to call their own - and the impregnability of the sanctuary tends to increase with organizational status. Three of the PDGs [CEOs] observed had soundproofed doors, great unwieldy things which were almost permanently closed."

If you don't have the good fortune to be the PDG, then your aim should be to get as close to his or her office as the hierarchy permits. This rule applies both vertically and horizontally.

Compartmentalisation including, even today, the use of double doors is also still evident in many of the larger German organisations. As Edward T Hall says, "the Germans think that open doors are sloppy and disorderly. To close the door preserves the integrity of the room and provides a protective boundary between people."

But the further German executives rise in the corporate hierarchy, the higher they are inclined to install themselves in the corporate HQ, assuming of course that it is a multi-storey building. In contrast to the French and the Belgians, they prefer an outside location with a view, preferably a corner office, as do the Anglo-Saxons.

Open-plan offices are a common feature of many Nordic countries, in line with their democratic approach to life generally. The Dutch aspire to the same degree of openness but, where they have doors, still tend to close them. Open-plan offices are supposed to be OK too in the UK, but meet a certain resistance at the more senior levels of many British hierarchies, possibly reflecting the moderately high power distance dimension detected by Hofstede.

Hierarchy in Britain, which since WWII has been more a matter of deference than formal company structuring, is now on the wane. It survives most virulently, as an extension of the country's addiction to class differences, in the form of separate dining rooms and washrooms for senior executives, middle management and workers.

A small yet significant aspect of heirarchy is the initial exchange of business cards. For some European cultures as well as the Japanese, this has symbolic significance which justifies a measured ritual. Rather than tuck your opposite numbers' cards away in your pocket, you will do well to be seen studying them carefully for all the signs of rank and authority, then placing them ceremoniously on the table in front of you for the duration of your meeting!

"In France the right of access to people or information is not a basic democratic principle. Having access is equated with power"

Barsoux and Lawrence, *Management in France*

"On one occasion one of my staff was speaking to a Norwegian colleague, who in mid-conversation suddenly said 'Good heavens, it's 3.30!' and put the phone down. This is not a very flexible attitude in a competitive world"

British business executive

"Since the French are licensed to be volatile, they sometimes use this trait as a weapon to keep subordinates off balance"

American publishing executive

"Your mother tongue is the language you count in"

Anonymous Dutch national

"'Why don't Swedes reply to letters and why don't they keep in touch?' was a constant cry"

Jean-Phillips Martinsson, *Swedes as Others see Them*

"Both Norwegians and Finns are rotten writers. We prefer the telephone to the letter. A telex is normally the nearest thing to a written confirmation. This system works well in Scandinavia, but I know that it irritates many German and French companies"

Finnish business executive

"When a Frenchman receives a letter and he is not in agreement, he does not respond. And that sends the message ' I do not agree '. On the other hand, when a German writes a letter to you and you do not respond, you are sending the signal ' I agree '. These are things you have to know"

André Leysen, Chairman, Gevaert NV, *Euromanagement*

The Nerve Ends

of communications
and consultants

The European trading cultures differ in their attitudes towards communications and the means available to them.

As an American CEO remarked back in the mid-60s, "an American executive tends to forget what he's said in a letter. A Frenchman never forgets what he's purposely left out." That sounds slightly cynical, but it has a ring of truth.

What comes across most clearly these days is that many French middle managers prefer not to commit themselves to paper in the first place, unless in self-defence: at a push, they will turn out a memo, but rarely a formal letter. As Barsoux and Lawrence say: "opting for the written form, particularly in companies with a mainly oral culture, is in itself a powerful signal - it can be seen as *une aggression* (an attack)." Such tactics are normally left to senior managers who use written communications to further their personal political aims rather than as a management tool.

A British business consultant offers another thought on the reticence to commit to paper: "The French in particular hate making business forecasts: the language makes it very difficult to find a shade of meaning to separate a business objective from a personal commitment" (as I have said elsewhere, the French regard the role and the person as separate and inviolate entities). The more nuanceful nature of English, with at least five times the vocabulary of French, makes it much easier for the British to weasel their way through...

On the other hand, if you're dealing with senior French executives, communication should be formal and **in writing**. In the words of a French lawyer: "Don't think you can communicate by phone. To the French, the telephone is only a tool to follow up a letter. The letter is never the tool to follow up a phonecall!" An international market researcher also comments how difficult it is to get a French response to a research study without making a formal approach.

The situation is markedly different in neighbouring countries. The British regard information as a tool rather than a commodity and, being less nervous about shared access, are in many companies already equipped with computer-based information systems. This in turn means that they make greater use of electronic communications - e-mail, voicemail, etc - than the business communities of the bigger Continental cultures.

Also in stark contrast to France, German business is only too happy to commit itself to writing. John Mole comments that "many German companies thrive on a massive amount of written communication, elaborating and confirming what has been discussed and agreed face-to-face. Such communication always used to be dictated and typed but with the escalating cost it is increasingly acceptable to use handwritten internal communication until electronic internal mail systems become more widespread."

He also makes a revealing comment when, in talking about German use of the telephone, he says that "Germans are more inhibited [than Latins], and especially on conference calls. They miss the cues and feedback and the setting." Cues in particular are vital in ensuring effective communication between and with Germans.

Further north, perhaps not surprisingly in view of the distances involved, electronic communications tends to take precedence over paper. Jean Phillips-Martinsson says that one of the most constant complaints to come out of her survey was that "Swedes rarely reply to letters, even to those requesting information as to whether their range includes specific products. If it did, they sometimes replied, but only after a considerable lapse of time. If it did not, they never troubled to reply to the enquiry."

Habert and Lillebø confirm that the same attitude prevails in Norway. In the words of a British businessman, "Norwegians appear most unwilling to put things in print. On one occasion I was exasperated at the lack of response from a Norwegian colleague on an important matter. I therefore wrote a mildly critical memo on the subject to him, and had him on the telephone as soon as he received it. It was clear to me that he was appalled at there being something critical about him in writing." The same attitude prevails in Finland too.

Stonewall or share?

In the matter of internal communications, a business feature describing Hofstede's work included a telling little story: "A large British company wanted to extend an advanced information system to its French operations. The system sent information directly to salesmen so that they could react quickly to customers' requirements and take fast action on pricing. The company was astonished when the system was furiously resisted by the top management of its French subsidiary. It had failed to take into account French sensitivity about the control of information, and the French reluctance to delegate power to juniors."

Of course, the reluctance of French managers to pass on data or knowhow in any form, electronic, paper-based or verbal, can be an extension of the principle of management by information retention. "People are reluctant to share their information", was the comment of one French industrialist talking to *The Economist*: "Managers in particular seem to think it gives them extra power."

Indeed 'management by information retention' rates as a recognised technique in France. But internal communications can also be bizarre in compartmentalised cultures like Germany. The Boehringer Ingelheim drug company failed to exploit new products coming out of its Japanese affiliate, simply because it didn't know they were there. Maybe the Japanese were as much to blame for this as the Germans.

Another example came to me when I was working as a consultant to a British inward investment agency, researching a story about the UK subsidiary of a well-known privately owned German corporation. When I approached the latter for their approval of the text, they told me they could not agree since the existence of the subsidiary was unknown to all except their top executives, for fear of disturbing the management/employee relationship. *Wir sind ja unter uns*!

Attitudes towards colleagues in the same industry also vary too, although all nationalities are wary about trading information with competitors. The British are particularly cautious, possibly in part because they do not have as highly developed a sense of trade or industry identity (or the associations to further it) as many Continentals. In the words of a Belgian woman executive in the travel trade, "the British are not very open, they regard almost everything as confidential."

155

Reporting on corruption in Italy in February 1994, *The Economist* quoted a survey undertaken among the younger members of Confindustria, the Italian industrialists' organisation:

"Some 85% of the 800 members of the association who were polled said that bribes used to be paid to secure public contracts before Milan magistrates launched their 'clean hands' inquiry in 1992. Although about 80% say that matters have improved since, they admit that the notorious *bustarelle* (envelopes) still change hands. And 13% say there has been no improvement at all. That proportion rises to 31.8% in the area the survey calls 'regions at risk' - Mafia-plagued Sicily, Calabria and Campania... In no other big western economy has corruption become so systematic.

... When asked whether they had ever been obliged to withdraw a tender for a public contract, 73% of the 286 people who answered this question said No. In Sicily, Calabria and Campania, only 42% said No. Of these, 23% said they were obliged to withdraw after threats. Another 35% in these 'regions at risk' said they had to withdraw as a result of pressure from 'channels other than organised crime'.

Given the high level of infiltration in local government by the Mafia (or its mainland cousins, the 'Ndrangheta in Calabria and the Camorra in Campania), the two figures can be added up. Thus 58% of small and medium-sized businesses in the three regions can be said to have suffered from coercion by the Mafia or its political friends.

... The survey attempts to gauge the spread of Mafia money - much of it from drug trafficking and racketeering - by asking the question: 'Are there companies in your area financed with money of dubious origin?' Nearly 62% of the sample said Yes. Of these, 55% said there were only a few, whereas 7% thought them 'numerous'. This, too, seems to be a national blight."

Curiously enough, the combination of an instinctive sense of socio-cultural solidarity and the prospect of an economy embattled in global competition predisposes the Germans, more than other Europeans, to share information with their fellow industrialists. Much of this information exchange is however formalised through the influential trade associations existing in most areas of German industry and commerce.

In external communications and attitudes toward the other 'estates' - academia and even the media - there are also marked differences in behaviour. British and Dutch managers tend to be relatively open, German and French managers closed.

A German international business journalist describes national responses to phone contact in the following terms: "German company spokespeople tend to be suspicious and over-cautious. The French are unhelpful, even bloody-minded, the Italians are just rude. Belgians? Impressionable, easy to scare. The best are the British, the Dutch and the Austrians, all of whom are generally very professional and helpful."

The French attitude reflects the perceived role of the media as attributed to a Michelin spokesperson by Barsoux and Lawrence: "Your job is to penetrate secrets. Ours is to safeguard the future of the Company."

Then there are variations in the links European business has with government. As must have been blindingly self-evident to everyone in recent times, there has been an intimate and almost symbiotic relationship in the Mediterranean countries of Europe - not just in Italy, but Spain and Greece as well. Evidence of similar practices also surface in Austria and Belgium from time to time.

That favours are exchanged for money is not unique to these countries of course. Moreover in some instances these relationships may have been well intentioned and even beneficial in 'getting things done'. Yet institutionalised mutual backscratching, as it has been practised in Italy (see box), is a scourge that businesspeople and consumers should be happy to say goodbye to.

While "French bosses find themselves involved with the state to a far greater extent than their Anglo-Saxon counterparts", as Barsoux and Lawrence point out, the relationship uses influence as its currency and not money. By comparison the business communities of Germany, The Netherlands, the Nordic countries and even Britain tend to keep a prudent distance between themselves and their rulers in every respect.

Confiding in consultants

Attitudes towards the use of independent consultants tend to vary from one European country to another. The Dutch, British and the Italians are generally enthusiastic users of their services (the good ones, that is), the others less so - particularly the Belgians, who are both suspicious of people selling ideas rather than merchandise and reluctant to pay for strategies which they are then obliged to respect to make them work.

In the opinion of a British consultant working in France, the French have been traditionally reticent on this score. He attributes this to a cultural attitude which contains, in varying degrees depending on the individual, strains of *orgeuil* or self-esteem (he or she knows it all better), natural suspicion and, in some cases, disillusionment with the over-theoretical approach of many French consultants. He concedes however that, here as elsewhere in Europe, the younger generations show a more open attitude.

From personal experience in two fields - executive search and public relations - the British and the Italians (those operating in a big business environment) are the most enthusiastic users of consultancy services, followed by the Dutch. The Germans do indeed draw on such services, but in a much more selective way and for specific types of assignment.

Other Latins do not share the Italians' enthusiasm for outside help but, then, most SME cultures share this reticence. The Catalan entrepreneur is typical of his kind when, as Martinez and Nueno point out, he shows a reluctance to seek help from other business professionals.

A few words may be appropriate here on European personnel selection techniques. Every nationality has its soft spot. In France, according to James Randi, ex-magician, conjurer and escape-artist, 10 per cent of companies insist on a handwriting test before hiring anyone and another 40 per cent make some use of the practice. Some of the French even think it is possible to find a missing person by waving a pendulum over a map.

A recently enacted French law reveals the true extent of these bizarre practices, which have included the use of astrologers, numerologists, clairvoyants and, last but by no means least, morphopsychologists (who judge your potential from your facial features). One French company even interprets the car licence plates of prospective employees in favour of those with 'magic numbers'.

Graphology and psychometric tests are also popular with many Belgian and German managers. As Max Messmer points out in his book, "some Belgian clients will not consider hiring a candidate without the graphologist's report on what his or her handwriting indicates about that job seeker's character."

There are German captains of industry who refuse to make strategic decisions until they have consulted their astrologers. Some Germans are devout believers in water divining - though not necessarily in a business context.

The English, James Randi suggests, have a fondness for communicating with the other world via a medium. He also says that the Americans tend to believe in anything that is scientific, while the Japanese believe in anything that is American...

"Formal training in France is largely irrelevant for those pegged for management and is reserved primarily for the lower echelons"

French lawyer

"For a team in the UK a uniform is important. In France, you belong to the team, but you don't want to be seen to belong"

Yves-Noel Derenne, Director of Human Resources, Eurotunnel

"You can't get the Dutch to compete with one another publicly"

British corporate psychologist, Paul Thorne

"In France, it would seem that the state has taken over the responsibility for training individuals to assume leadership positions"

Barsoux and Lawrence, *Management in France*

"Small talk touching on the favourite issues of football and politics must be handled with care in Spain"

Georgina Power, *The European*

"When I go to Holland, I'm lucky if I'm treated to a sandwich and milk in the office. When the Dutch come here, they arrive just in time for lunch, expect to be taken out - and there's always more than one of them"

Belgian subsidiary manager of Dutch parent company

"When the Wall Street Journal *asked a Dutch chief executive why his company was not entering the German market, he replied, 'Because we don't like Germans'"*

The Journal of European Business

The Nerve Ends

of the professional
and the private

Obviously one should be cautious in imposing one's own *idées réçues* on such intimate matters as training and self-improvement on others, especially those from particularly alien or ethnocentric cultures. Yet, equally obviously, this **cannot** be so obvious - to judge from the mistakes that most of us make from time to time, myself included.

France is clearly a particularly ethnocentric culture. The word 'ethnocentric' is inaccurate since, first, France is hardly an ethnic entity (as mentioned earlier, Luigi Barzini maintains that nearly 50 per cent of the current French population have Germanic genes!) and, secondly, France is the example *par excellence* of a successful centuries-long conspiracy to create a culture where no culture existed (the embryonic nation emerged on the ashes of **two** cultures, the *langue d'oc* and the *langue d'oil*). But that has little to do with business...

The present reality is that French people have to be handled with due and proper respect - they take themselves very seriously. So don't treat them like children. And in particular, don't treat them *en masse*. The French may have behaved *en masse* during their Revolution (to the detriment of most of the rest of Europe) but, in normal times like the present, they prefer to be treated as individuals.

The ego of the average French person is inviolable. Management specialists say it is difficult to get French executives to accept training in interviewing techniques: this is an insult to their self-esteem. They are sensitive to anything that challenges their *amour-propre*.

This sensitivity may explain in part the French insistence that authority is vested in the individual's role or function and not in his or her person. By this device, the person remains intact.

Personal sensitivity is, indeed, a major consideration in any Latin country and explains why Anglo-Saxon appraisal systems, as used in MBO (management by objectives) schemes, are difficult to apply. Speaking of Italians, John Mole says that "formal personal appraisal is very difficult for either side to manage, as is any direct criticism, unless it is in the context of a recognised personal relationship." The same applies to Spain.

In formal training, where the French and other Latins feel perfectly comfortable with an *ex cathedra* approach from their instructors, the British and the Nordics instinctively reject the teacher who talks down to them and respect the one who says "I don't know". Preferred teaching philosophies and structures differ markedly between countries.

In his book *Cultures and Organizations* Geert Hofstede speaks of his experience of lecturing on an International Teachers Program: "Most Germans... favor structured learning situations with precise objectives, detailed assignments, and strict timetables. They like situations in which there is one correct answer which they can find. They expect to be rewarded for accuracy. Their preferences are typical for strong uncertainty avoidance countries. Most British participants on the other hand despise too much structure. They like open-ended learning situations with vague objectives, broad assignments, and no timetables at all. The suggestion that there could be only one correct answer is taboo for them. They expect to be rewarded for originality. Their reactions are typical for countries with weak uncertainty avoidance."

The laid-back attitude of the British is evident to one of their number who trains international groups in the art of crisis management. He claims it takes his fellow-countryfolk time to take things seriously, with a consequent lack of preparation. By comparison, the French tackle the matter in hand with great verve and expense of energy, often thwarting their own intentions by an excess of cartesianism.

Low-key, high-key...

American companies that have expected their French employees to wear sloganed T-shirts at company conferences or, even worse, to sing the company chant every morning (I lie not) have been rewarded with at best insubordination or at worst mass desertions.

In his book *Managing the Multinational*, Samuel Humes cites such an example: "General Electric's experience in the 1988 takeover of the French medical equipment maker Compagnie Générale de Radiologie (CGR) demonstrates the hazards of even the most well-intended efforts. At an initial management training session GE gave out GE T-shirts with a

The human resources director of a major international consultancy and training company, someone who also spends a lot of his time teaching classes of various nationalities, comments on the need to nuance the educational approach:

The British: I float an idea for discussion, we thrash it out, come out with a general consensus where the wisdom is evident and then stop. The British do not want a cast-iron conclusion: they feel confident in interpreting the consensus.

The Dutch: Again I come up with an idea, we have a discussion, but I'm expected to wind up with a firm and clearly defined resolution. They want **the** answer: 'this is the way it's done'.

The Germans: They're like the Dutch, only want to be even more definitive. You have a discussion, you agree a solution, and that's it! It's set in concrete. There's no further discussion, they go away and do it.

The French: You have to appeal to their intellect, invoke the words and thoughts of their philosophers, De Tocqueville and the like.

The Swiss: Very closed minds, introverted. On matters of management improvement, they consider themselves almost above the law.

The Austrians: More open, charming, very laid back, proud of their history...

The Italians: Difficult to arrive at any final conclusion - the arguments go on and on, get noisier and noisier. I end up shouting!

The Nordics: Generally one of the easiest groups - or group of groups - to train. Very open-minded, good in discussion. The problem is you will have a lot of difficulty in getting much participation if the class has a lot of Finns in it...

note: 'Wear this to show you are a member of the team'. The move generated resentment."

The Germans, less openly intractable than the French, greet such transatlantic initiatives with a more passive but equally effective resistance, based on the reasonable belief that business is serious stuff.

The British, though natural sceptics, are a little less resistant and have even been known to respond positively to Japanese management by example. This, however, happens more often at shopfloor level and is an unspoken comment on the abysmal management standards practised in the past by their fellow-countryfolk.

Dutch people are brought up not to stand out in a crowd. I had dramatic evidence of this when talking to a group of Dutch students. On asking how many of them had had the opportunity to read my first book (and knowing full well that at least 20 of them had already done so), I was met with a determined silence. Only afterwards, when talking with their professor, did I understand that Dutch students do **not** show off in front of their classmates.

A British marketing consultant trained Dutch and British groups in brainstorming techniques. He found that, when asked to list all the applications they could think of for a variety of everyday objects, the Dutch typically came up with less than a quarter of the British contribution. However, when the Dutch discovered they were only expected to say **how many** applications they had thought of (and not actually describe them), they were just as prolific. The problem was more one of modesty and fear of criticism than of creativity. As he said, "the British don't mind making fools of themselves in public..."

International management trainers confirm that Dutch nationals have difficulty with role-playing as a training technique, precisely because their culture has taught them not to compete with one another publicly. As an American puts it, "you're simply not allowed to 'win'." Many of them even seem to be nervous about using the telephone: there may be a connection (no pun intended).

This degree of restraint, which is particularly evident in 'start-up' situations before personal relationships and roles

166

have been clearly established, is remarkable - particularly so since, once relationships are established, Dutch people can be as bossy and dogmatic as everyone else, and if anything more so.

Hofstede throws some light on the low-key behaviour of his fellow-countryfolk in a classic start-up situation, i.e. as job applicants: "They write modest and usually short CVs, counting on the interviewer to find out by asking how good they really are. They expect an interest in their social and extra-curricular activities during their studies. They are very careful not to be seen as braggarts and not to make promises they are not absolutely sure they can fulfill."

Later on, Hofstede quotes what he describes as "an untranslatable expression" used by Dutch people, *'doe maar gewoon, dan doe je al gek genoeg'*, which notwithstanding he manages to render as "just behave like everybody else, you're ridiculous enough anyway"! According to a specialist in crisis communications, however, prudence does not inhibit some of their number from standing up in training courses and asking silly questions just to get themselves noticed.

But that seems to be the exception rather than the rule. In the words of William Shetter, an American observer of the Dutch scene[33]: "Today Dutch people still tend to be distrustful of too-conspicuous individual achievement or even 'show', to dislike anything perceived as excessive display of affluence, to maintain a discreet public reserve that meticulously respects the privacy of others, to accept outsiders readily and unquestioningly, and above all to cherish the forms of social organization that help assure all this."

Wim Kan, a Dutch entertainer, summed it all up in something like the following words: "We have no balconies [it's a fact] so we have no revolutions. Our balconies are 'at the back'."

Similar attitudes are found in the Nordic countries, which rub shoulders with The Netherlands at the lower end of Hofstede's masculinity dimension. Richard Mead[34] quotes Jacob Vedel-Petersen, director of the Institute for Social Science Research in Copenhagen: "We don't admire big stars or heroes very much, the man in the street is our hero." Even the Swedish Prime Minister, as Mead adds, is required by law to open his official mail to any citizen anxious to read it.

Americans find the generally low-key Nordic approach perplexing. Jean Phillips-Martinsson describes a typical situation where a Swede stonewalls the attempts of his American visitor to draw him out: "This kind of behaviour flusters the American who is looking for a dialogue, not a monologue. He's longing to be asked some questions so he can show the photographs which he carries in his wallet. The Swede, on the other hand, brought up not to ask such questions, is feeling out of place."

As for the Finns, well, in the words of a British multinational executive "they're loners, they're simply not good at team games."

All of this is a far cry from the relation-oriented traditions of many European countries, particularly the Latin ones. Moreover such attitudes go back a long way. Hofstede cites the case of Jean Baptiste Bernadotte, the French general 'headhunted' for the Swedish throne, who gave his inaugural address in his best Swedish (the thought of a Frenchman talking Swedish almost defies imagination). His valiant efforts only provoked laughter from the assembly and he swore never to speak Swedish again. What is surprising in this cameo is not the Frenchman's reaction which is quite understandable (nobody in France had ever dared laugh at him), but the fact that, even on such an august occasion, the power distance dimension of the Swedes was so low that they couldn't restrain themselves from laughing!

Although eastern Europe is outside the remit of this book, it is interesting to note Richard Mead's comment that, in Russia, "bragging about your achievements is perceived as placing yourself above the collective group and is shameful. A Russian immigrant to the United States was frequently reduced to tears by the humiliation of having to extol her own achievements in job interviews." Shades of The Netherlands!

Many Germans in business are equally reticent about self-display or boasting. Yet, when invited to introduce him or herself to a group, in the words of the US magazine *Trade & Culture*, "the German will begin at the beginning of his or her life, and proceed step by step to the present with a relatively

168

detailed catalogue of formal educational degrees and successive corporate titles." As German industrial policy guru Konrad Seitz said: "Germans are more thorough than fast".

'La poire et le fromage'

Continentals generally prefer to make a clear and sometimes absolute distinction between their professional and their private lives. Even work-oriented Nordics consider their families and leisure time sacrosanct and, while they will invite the visiting executive into their homes, will not appreciate your discussing business out of office hours.

Speaking of the Germans, John Mole says: "There is a clear demarcation between private and business life. They leave work as punctually as they arrive and rarely take work home. They do not like being called at home on business unless there is a very good reason... Germans have a strong sense of privacy and their protective shell extends much further into public life than in many other countries."

This protective shell can even totally encompass public or professional life, and not just in the sense that some Germans are still great believers in double doors. Making an appointment can be a very casual thing in a 'polychronic' and relaxed Mediterranean country, and a very formal one in a 'monochronic' country like Germany.

An Italian businessman found this out to his cost when visiting a customer in the Stuttgart area. Having travelled a considerable distance at his own expense for a meeting with the production manager of the manufacturing subsidiary of a major German group, he discovered that another of the group's plants located only a few kilometers away could also be a prospect for his company's products. When he proposed to drop in that same day since he was in the area, he was told it was inappropriate and that he should contact for an appointment on his return to Italy! To an opportunistic Italian, this simply didn't make sense.

The protective shell is also evident in initial contacts with Spaniards. Too many personal questions too soon in the relationship can make your opposite number distinctly uncomfortable. Once the relationship is established, however, a high degree of intimacy in such matters is permitted.

In fact, when socialising in a professional context, the Spanish as much as the French and even the British (as the closest to the Americans), consider a relaxed conversation about current affairs, the arts or sports to be a normal extension to a business relationship. Yet, warns a Spanish recruiter, "the Spanish are very spontaneous and impetuous. Interviewees need to avoid passion-awakening topics of conversation that could lead to confrontations". Politics and bullfighting could be two of them, maybe even football...

Most importantly, never (even with most English people) enquire into such intimate matters as the money your host earns. Generally on the European continent, such things are taboo: speaking of France, Barsoux and Lawrence highlight "the Catholic reticence to talk about money." A top executive's income may be a matter of public knowledge in the US, thanks to the proxy statement attached to the employer's annual report, but elsewhere this is a closely kept private secret. Germany, for example, only requires disclosure of the aggregate payments to members of a public company's management board.

At least you know where you are in France. In the words of Glen Fisher, an American academic[35], "the French present variations from American themes by differentiating more carefully between their public and private worlds, by seeing themselves as people of thought and reason, and by taking history more seriously."

While such personal matters may be off-limits, it is perfectly OK in Germany to talk business over a business lunch or dinner. In France, on the other hand, and to a lesser extent in other Latin countries, even this may be taboo on such occasions. In the words of a French journalist, "during this time the protagonists avoid, at all costs, talking business."

So the safest thing, if invited out to lunch or dinner in France, is to leave it to your host to bring up the subject first. This will most likely happen towards the end of the meal - 'entre la poire et le fromage', as the French say. You will hardly notice the change as the conversation flows gently from social topics to professional matters - so be prepared!

It may seem kafkaesque but there are some business people, French in particular, who don't even want to be asked what they do for a living! So the advice throughout must be that, when moving out of the professional into the particular, don't ask questions, just let people offer you the answers.

Various matters of etiquette apply when you are invited to your business partner's home. The choice of what you bring as a gift for your host's wife is a tricky one for a start: there is no such thing as a universal language of flowers, despite the advertising claims, and the same species can have dramatically different implications from one culture to another. But there are plenty of books in the 'when in Rome, do as the Romans do' category to guide you.

Don't take it for granted in any case that you will be invited into a European's home. Many cultures are circumspect on this matter. Take it as a great privilege if it happens to you in one of the Nordic countries. Your host's wife, who almost certainly has a professional activity of her own, will have worked very hard to make you welcome (including spring-cleaning the house) and there are some large Nordic companies that have a corporate policy of not even allowing home entertainment of foreign guests.

Like flowers, the use of humour is a hazardous process, particularly in a business context. The Dutch say that, when talking in public, the British always start off with a joke, the Germans with a definition, and the Dutch with an apology... for their poor English or their poor German (which is a joke in itself). The best thing is to assume that everything being said is serious, and just laugh politely if your host laughs first.

As in many other things, however, it is the Irish who have the last laugh. One country where you can afford to mix the personal with the professional is Ireland. A canny multinational manager, sent to run his company's local subsidiary, found there was only one thing he needed to do to cement customer relationships: whenever a director of a customer company died, he made a point of turning up in person at the funeral!

In-late 1993 international management consultants Peter Chadwick interviewed senior executives of 323 large to medium size companies in Britain, France and Germany on quality and performance monitoring. Key findings of the study included :

Systematically monitoring customer satisfaction

Britain : 92 %   France : 80 %   Germany : 78 %

Informing all employees of customer service performance

Britain : 44 %   France : 50 %   Germany : 14 %

[So not all French companies practise 'management by information retention' !]

Using statistical performance measurement techniques

Britain : 63 %   France : 59 %   Germany : 72 %

Setting performance targets for business departments

Britain : 75 %   France : 40 %   Germany : 75 %

Meeting time-to-market / product development targets

Britain : 59 %   France : 73 %   Germany : 76 %

Training employees in a variety of skills

Britain : 68 %   France : 82 %   Germany : 66 %

Using employee suggestion schemes

Britain : 68 %   France : 45 %   Germany : 82 %

Reducing the number of suppliers

Britain : 45 %   France : 33 %   Germany : 29 %

"British companies appeared to be the most advanced at having initiatives to monitor customer satisfaction, improve quality, reduce cycle times, use cross functional teams, and reduce the number of suppliers. German companies appeared to be the most advanced in taking steps to set performance targets, measure performance through statistical methods, and consult their employees' views through suggestion schemes. French companies were markedly advanced only in providing multi-skills training for their employees... "

Source : Peter Chadwick, *Satisfying the Customer - Fact or Fiction ?*

"The British can be tricky, putting up a smokescreen then springing something on you - sometimes naively"

Belgian marketing director

"They talk a lot, but they do listen"

Belgian woman executive speaking of the French

"The Spanish skill of persuasion, face to face, is hard to match"

John Parry, *The European*

"In Sweden negotiations and decision-making go together. So what takes the Swedes one week to do takes the Norwegians four weeks. The Norwegians are better at thinking through alternatives. But the Swedes are better at making decisions"

Swedish business executive

"It's the French way of doing things"

GATT official commenting on Gallic stonewalling tactics

"I have found in Norwegians a tendency to be trusting"

Canadian business lawyer

"Most important emotional messages at a negotiating table - like those conveying friendship or anger, confidence or mistrust - are expressed nonverbally by gestures, tone of voice, or facial expressions"

Jeswald W Salacuse, *Making Global Deals*[36]

"It is very seldom that high-level business negotiations on the Norwegian side are left to one individual; it is very much teamwork, which reduces chances of misunderstanding. That is, by the way, confusing to the French negotiator, often used to concentrating all decision power in his hands, who finds it difficult to identify his Norwegian counterpart across the table"

French business executive

"The French go to find out what the boss has decided to do"

Sir Alistair Morton, CEO of Eurotunnel

Chapter 5

THE CRUNCH POINTS

negotiation

The negotiating table, more than any other setting, provides the classic *ad hoc* opportunity for the emergence of national characteristics and for culture clash: unexpected responses, linguistic and gestural confusion, dissemblance using language as a cover - in short differing value, negotiating and communications systems.

Such problems are implicit even in in-house negotiations, where those involved are presumed to be 'on the same side'. So when adversaries face one another across the negotiating table, they are inevitably magnified to the point that they can easily disrupt what should be smooth proceedings.

The problems start with preconceptions. Referring in his book *International Negotiation*[35] to a study undertaken for the US Department of State's Foreign Service Institute, Dr Glen Fisher says: "No other set of psychological factors was mentioned as frequently by persons who contributed to this study as the perceptions their counterparts held of their country's international position or of their special qualities as a nation."

Prabhu Guptara, an international management consultant, describes typical expectations of behaviour in commercial negotiations: "The English are perceived as sociable, flexible, and under-prepared... Germans have a reputation for coming to negotiations thoroughly prepared, of bidding strongly and early, and of being unlikely to move from their bids once made... The French, too, are perceived as firm. They tend to adopt a broad-front approach, going from an outline agreement to an agreement in principle, to heads of agreement, etc... Northern Europeans come across as more shy."

The social being beneath

In potentially high-tension situations like international negotiations, it is impossible to divorce the professional persona entirely from the social being beneath. So the first consideration in understanding different cultures' negotiating behaviour is to examine the underlying behavioural predispositions. As Edward Hall makes clear (see Chapter 2), Latins tend to be more relation-oriented than Germanics, with the result that the Latin approach is likely to be more empathetic and, in the wrong circumstances, more antipathetic.

Personal affinities clearly influence the outcome of bargaining sessions. Various studies have shown that interpersonal attraction increases the likelihood of a satisfactory deal for both parties. In some cases this is more or less synonymous with cultural similarity, which suggests that negotiations among Germanics stand a greater chance of success than negotiations between Germanics and Latins, for example.

British research psychologist Peter Collett, in his fascinating book *Foreign Bodies*[37], offers a deeper insight into the social predispositions of Europe's cultures: "One of the reasons why the English are so reserved is that they have a deep-seated desire not to impose themselves on other people, and not to be imposed upon by others. This trait, however, is not unique to the English, and it can be found in various other parts of Europe, including Finland, Sweden, Norway, and the north of Germany - in fact, everywhere where people are more concerned about not being disliked, rather than being liked. The motivating force behind interpersonal relations in these countries is a desire to avoid the negative consequences of other people's disapproval. This is quite the opposite to what one finds in the south of Europe, where people are motivated by the pursuit of approval." What vast perspectives this intriguing observation opens up!

Collett is certainly right to put the Nordics high on his list of those anxious to avoid disapproval. Yet, according to linguistics experts Penelope Brown and Stephen Levinson, there is an even subtler difference between the English (Collett rightly eschews the term 'British' in this context) and the Finns. Where the English use 'positively oriented' politeness - words like "excuse me", "if I may say so" and the very significant word "actually" - the Finns prefer a 'negatively oriented' avoidance-based strategy.

So Anglo-Saxon politeness seems extravagant and unnecessary to the Finns. For their part, the Finns don't want to seem rude, they just say nothing. If they bump into one another in the street, they tend at best to say "O ho !"

Jean Phillips-Martinsson records an interesting parallel in her book *Swedes as Others see Them*: "The lack of a word for 'please' in the Swedish language means that you [the Swedes] are inclined to exclude it even in English. This omission can well account for your reputation of being curt and giving orders".

178

Such considerations complicate enormously the task of cross-table understanding in international negotiations. After all, the English and the Nordics tend to think that, culturally speaking, they are more or less on the same side. How much more perplexing when one is dealing with demonstrably different cultures!

Even variations in how cultures express themselves physically can get in the way of an interchange. As Peter Collett says: "Basically the phonetics of English, especially the vowel sounds, do not encourage the vigorous facial movements and apparent emotion that happens with French speakers. You just can't speak French with a stiff upper lip..."

And, to complicate matters still further, everything ultimately depends on the intentions of those involved. Is Party A out to achieve a genuine consensus with Party B. Is Party B out to take Party A for a ride? Probably the truth lies halfway between but, again, the element of the unknown is immeasurable.

When they 're playing it straight...

The **British**, with their weak uncertainty avoidance, are indeed flexible in their approach to negotiations though, if properly trained for the job, they can be exceedingly skillful and tough. Unfortunately for them, this is not always the case and Prabhu Guptara's comment on being 'under-prepared' is fully justified (he, like Collett, refers to the 'English' but, on this rare occasion, I think all the inhabitants of the British Isles can be included in the judgment).

It is as if weak uncertainty avoidance positively encourages the British executive to walk into the negotiating room under-prepared: he is relishing the challenge of displaying his native quick-wittedness and spontaneity. Moreover, by not preprogramming himself to an assumed situation and course of action, he is allowing full rein to these qualities.

Despite weak uncertainty avoidance, there is a limit to how far British negotiators will go. A researcher, Klaus Schmidt, comments that among the British, "a quiet, confident demeanor is... essential. In business, this demeanor is characterized by a measured approach. Emotions are vented cautiously." Dr Allan Hjorth of the Copenhagen Business

"I cannot determine a person's culture from the way he or she negotiates, and I certainly cannot predict someone's style of negotiating simply by knowing the nationality. Whether the attitude is, 'I cannot win', 'you must not win', 'we must both be satisfied', or whatever, depends on the individual more than on the culture.

Still, I do sense differences among European cultures - in the role of interpersonal attraction, in the importance of money as a criterion, and in the perception of when an agreement has been reached.

Interpersonal attraction - which can enhance the level of trust and the desire to reach agreement - seems to play a more important role with Latins and Anglo-Saxons than with Germanics. As a matter of principle, Nordics tend to avoid personal conflict and prefer neutral, logical solutions over having to negotiate. The money issue also arises with them: the suggestion that a deal will lead to 'getting rich' may be viewed as an excessive or even negative outcome.

Nordics, Germans and central/eastern Europeans tend to want a single 'best solution'. Failing that, the unattractive alternative seems to be a 'less best solution' or compromise, often leading to negotiating strategies which appear outright competitive. Conversely, the Anglo-Saxons, French and other Europeans seem comfortable with multiple or incremental solutions. I also notice that Germans get introspective when I disagree on the issue or a solution, perhaps raising doubts about their competence ('am I failing?'), and their negotiating strategy becomes more adversarial. I wonder whether the apparent attack is more of a defense.

Communication - the use or non-use of information, what is communicated and how - differs consistently across cultures. Notably the French and French-speaking Belgians seem to regard it as a precious commodity, to be dispensed sparingly. This may reflect the principle of 'management by information retention', but it also signals a reluctance to indulge in self-disclosure. It is as if the French have an 'intellectual intimate zone' comparable to the physical 'bubble of space' that is so important to northern Europeans. The British, by contrast, use the richness of their language - sometimes to communicate, often to maneuvre others toward an 'inescapable conclusion'. Many of them are schooled in rhetoric and tend to enjoy lengthy debate. The inclusion of personal or emotional data in negotiating shades from negative to affirmative, as one moves from north to south across the Continent.

The final difference - when a negotiation is finished - occurs when one party believes agreement is reached while the other believes the contract is not yet clear and specific. For example, Greeks report dislike of detailed written contracts, still relying on personal word of honor. They prefer incremental agreements, proceeding 'plank by plank' to build a solid bridge. While looking carefully at every step, they often do not articulate where they want to be at the end of the process.

Ironically, as a common law people, the British prefer lengthy written contracts which spell out the many consequences of failure to fulfill terms. In between, the relative importance of the 'agreement' versus the 'contract' varies. In contractual cultures attorneys negotiate, in deal-making cultures the active parties negotiate.

What do these differences mean? As simplified generalizations, they alert me to examine my own assumptions and strategies in negotiating, and to learn how to adapt to other perceptions. I find it much more satisfying to negotiate 'in parallel' with my counterparts, so we can focus on the issues, rather than unwittingly competing over how to negotiate."

American human relations consultant, **Bob Ward**

School makes the same point: "In Britain there is a dislike of open conflict: everything is done on a more low-key level."

Terms can be 'low-key' too, posing the question as to whether the British really want the deal to succeed. Suppression of emotions can also lead to situations where the British are ultimately judged hypocritical by the other side...

Various Continental observers make the comment that the British are not very open to other people's ideas. A French businessman remarks that "when you're outlining something to them, you get the feeling they're thinking up reasons why your proposal is unacceptable!" This comment was echoed by a Belgian.

When it comes to committing conclusions to paper, the British are anything but vague. Most Continentals are astonished at the lengths they will go to, as the comments of this Belgian woman company director show: "The British are great ones for detail, very finicky. They want everything on paper, and every line of a contract has to be absolutely right." They make the Americans, by comparison, look almost indecently laid back.

In stark contrast to British behaviour, the **German** approach to negotiations is systematic and sequential. As an article in the US magazine *Trade & Culture* stated pointedly: "It's critical to realize that, since Germans place value on past achievements, they are often somewhat leery of new products and processes, and want to have all the details before trying out something new. As a result, you should examine all sides of a particular issue in your presentation, perhaps even describing the ideas you rejected, in order to prove that you ultimately chose the logically defensible path." And, further on: "To be convincing to a German, an argument must be *schlüssig* - so complete and logically constructed with solid facts that the conclusion is simply unavoidable."

Speaking of doing business in Frankfurt, journalist Alan Tillier quotes the comments of an American international executive. "It's counterproductive, possibly fatal, for a visitor to say, in effect: 'let's sign this - I have a flight to catch.' That won't move the German: he is likely to schedule another meeting. Details and more details - that is the *Leitmotiv*."

Author Philip Glouchevitch feels compelled to offer the following advice when negotiating with Germans: "Do not interrupt the person with whom you are speaking even if you have figured out what he wants to say. Let the person get there by himself; otherwise he may be disoriented for the rest of the conversation because you have broken the coherence and continuity of his speech." Some uncharitable foreigners describe this syndrome as tunnel vision, but that would be seriously underestimating the Germans: it is 'lock-on' radar.

In fact the Germans are as at ease with silence as are the Finns, and that's saying a lot! This can be a valuable attribute when negotiating. Latins, and even the British, get much more edgy - and run the risk of giving away more than they want to.

This stoical attitude is even evident when Germans have something they are anxious to sell. A management consultant quoted by Richard Mead says that, in Germany, you should "expect to settle for a difference of 10% on the price. The Germans *don't negotiate* [my italics], they start off by finding out precisely what you want, then quote the price." They sound as inflexible as the Swedes...

In fact a number of studies have suggested that, of the key European trading nations, the Germans are the toughest in their negotiating stances and the least influenced by interpersonal attraction. Klaus Schmidt found that "during negotiations, the German will keep his distance. He feels a personal relationship might interfere with the performance of his job."

This is borne out by the experience of a Danish marketing director working with a multinational in the automotive field. "I was astonished by the way my German sales manager tackled one of his distributors. He said 'I'm sorry, Doktor Schultz, evidently you don't understand. I will say it to you one more time very slowly'. It was said calmly and coldly, without any attempt to sweeten the pill."

Once the deal is done, the Germans habitually stick emphatically to their word. A Dutch managing director comments that "when the Germans have agreed a deal, it stays a deal. It's not the same with the French: they may decide to renegotiate, either because they've changed their minds or because they hadn't looked carefully enough at the specifications..."

Negotiations for the **French** have a social as well as a professional dimension. A British business consultant in Paris explains: "One of the features of doing business in France is that, before the French are willing to consider your deal seriously, they have to decide whether or not you are the sort of person they want to do business with. There is nothing chauvinistic in this - they simply expect you to go about things in exactly the same way."

Yet, once they have given you their vote, the French will bend over backwards to accommodate you. Referring to their legendary creative skills, a Belgian marketing executive says "they will even be extremely creative in finding excuses for you, to explain why things are not being done the way they should be done!" He adds that, from his substantial experience, "the French are becoming more thorough and professional than the Germans in negotiating contracts. They're well prepared, they know what they're talking about, and they're intelligent. You have to reason carefully with them and, if necessary, embellish what you're proposing..."

As past masters in the art of stage management, the French have negotiating techniques entirely of their own. Where the Germans rely on substance and the British on style, the French rely on effect. Their approach is likely to be inventive and challenging. As Jean Phillips-Martinsson points out: "When a Frenchman says '*Non, c'est impossible*' (no, it's impossible), you often take him at his face value. What the Frenchman really means is 'start convincing me'..."

In negotiations the French will often play along the opposition, almost for the fun of it, and then make a theatrical last-minute concession (what some foreign observers refer to naughtily as the 'Fashoda crisis syndrome'[*]). The most important thing is that they should not be **seen** to be capitulating.

Being intellectually hyperactive, the French revel in the negotiating process. As an American found out to his cost, "a basic rule with the French is that several people talk at

---

[*] Fashoda was the scene of an incident in Upper Egypt in 1898, when a small troop of Frenchmen held up a British army for six weeks before, on receipt of instructions from Paris, withdrawing precipitously and without loss.

the same time, with ever-increasing speed and volume." This observation is echoed by Klaus Schmidt, who says that the French "will interrupt communications with countless arguments."

Also, to quote the words of a Belgian multinational executive, "the French spend a lot of time and energy talking around a problem rather than concentrating on the solution." It was an American CEO who commented that, if Shakespeare had been a Frenchman, he would have had Hamlet say "To be or not to be, that is the question. *But the question is badly formulated.*"

A French executive confirms these opinions, with typically Gallic elegance and succinctness: "The Frenchman is often more interested in the way the negotiations develop than in the results." A Danish marketing executive interprets this quite simply in terms of the fact that the French "lack listening skills." An international consultant active in the regional development field is more emphatic: "The French are like the Japanese, they say 'yes' and do nothing." An American multinational sales director puts it differently with the words "they are not easy to convince." Clearly, everyone finds the French difficult...

Much of course can be explained by the severity of French logic, which not only baffles foreigners but also complicates the negotiating process for the French too. In his book Glen Fisher states: "To the French, a well-reasoned position does not call for compromise unless the reasoning is faulty. And that can be discussed. Even when a compromise is pragmatically although reluctantly reached, the French negotiator still gains some satisfaction in recalling the correctness of the preferred uncompromised position."

A German vice president with the European HQ of a major US multinational (who happens to be sympathetic to the French, being married to one of their number) concludes that "negotiations with the French can be very time-consuming, they keep on questioning things, they go into unnecessary details, and their decision-making criteria can often seem very strange to a foreigner."

Magnus Morgan, a Swedish executive search consultant, voices a more partisan point of view: "If you deal with the

A British business consultant in Paris describes the difference between British and French negotiating tactics:

"The Anglo-Saxon deal is input-dominated: the objective is to give up as little as possible, to put as little as possible into the kitty before the other fellow signs. It follows that the happier **you** [the Brit] are with the deal, the more likely it is that the other fellow will become unhappy with it as time goes by, hence the legal emphasis on contractual escape clauses.

The French deal, on the other hand, is output-dominated in the sense that it is based not on compromise, but on each side's continuing to pursue its own objectives while benefiting from the fact that many of these are shared by the partner. The French deal tends to be loose, optimistic. It very often does not envisage failure at all, and the only negative note may be the naming of a mutually acceptable referee to take care of disputes."

• • •

"A British real estate developer had a very good deal in the major provincial city of Lyons. But he needed bridging finance, and so he went to a Paris bank. The bank's executive started his speech - and it was no less - with the ominous words, *en principe* ('in principle'). Fifteen minutes or so later he uttered the magic words *mais, en pratique* ('but in practice'). Blinking in the sunshine outside, the British developer shook his head in disbelief and asked the interpreter plaintively: 'Well, do I have the loan, or don't I?'. Well, yes, he did have it - but he had first to pay the price, a philosophical statement of the difference between principle and practice."

Alan Tillier, IHT Guide to Business Travel: Europe

French, it's never straight, the turf is turned over 15 times, and you suddenly get a change of direction. It takes a lot of emotional involvement."

"They'll run you over several times just for the sake of it and for the pleasure of knowing that they haven't given anything away free." Yet in fairness, where the English will take what you say at its face value, the French will quite rightly probe and question to be sure they understand exactly what you mean.

Negotiations with the **Spanish** tend to be measured, gentlemanly and at times rather inconclusive. Like the French, they prefer to develop a relationship as a preliminary step, rather than as part of the negotiation process itself. Helen Wattley Ames comments that "when Spaniards meet someone for the first time to plan, bargain or negotiate, they want to take the measure of their counterpart and decide whether they would like to do business with him or her." Disinclined to go straight into the ring, "the Spaniard would rather get acquainted by discussing world politics or soccer or the beauty of the Pyrenees" (not Spanish politics you note).

So much depends with the Spaniard on the establishment of a personal rapport. Once this exists, no culture is more open to a relationship of mutual trust. Helen Wattley Ames, writing for her compatriots, explains that "an American entering into contract negotiations may be disconcerted at the amount of information that is taken for granted or left unclear. Spaniards often feel there is no need to pore over details, since everything can be worked out satisfactorily as long as the person one is dealing with is *de confianza*."

Of course language barriers tend to complicate things, accentuating the impression that Spanish people are aloof, which they certainly are not. But José Antonio de Urbina[38] makes the point that the Spanish could benefit from spending more time listening to what the other party has to say. The process of developing consensus can be a slow one - Glen Fisher talks of the Spanish tradition of placing emphasis on contemplation and intuition - but it is one that is ultimately likely to be productive.

As the relationship develops, inhibitions melt away and your Spanish counterpart is likely to become increasingly emphatic. Prolixity is one of the features of Spanish involvement in an issue. Other characteristics are described by Helen Wattley Ames: "Spaniards interrupt speakers without intending offense, and speakers raise their voices in the face of attempted interruption or disagreement. Therefore, Spanish negotiations, like Spanish conversation, can easily become loud." Depending on circumstances, Spaniards can be impressively silent or impressively noisy. As VS Pritchett said: "The fact is that they are people of excess: excessive in silence and reserve, excessive in speech when they suddenly fly into it..." Natural suspicion gives way to natural enthusiasm.

As for the **Italians**, they of course have their inimitable way of negotiating. As many business people have noted, they do what they want to. They will argue at length, disagree theatrically, appear to compromise, leave the conference room and then rethink their whole strategy in front of the espresso machine.

As a British consultant who works for some major Italian corporations points out: "Italians rarely make decisions openly in meetings. They do this as a private clique in the washroom or whatever. Then they come back into the meeting room and go through the motions, but everyone knows that the decision has already been made. Where the British record decisions the Italians, for obvious reasons, prefer not to."

This does not mean to say that negotiations are doomed to failure. Consensus is perfectly possible, with the Italians honouring their own interests and, as often as not, those of the others as well. The American CEO of a major multinational comments: "The Italians are extremely competent in business. They know what is possible and will concede when necessary. Their behaviour is of course conditioned by the fact that, historically, they have been in a state of constant rebellion against the Church and the State." And, as an afterthought, "they're natural-born cheats".

By way of elaboration, in his book The Art of International Negotiations[39], British management expert F Posses says: "... the striking of hands, as amongst the Italians, should not be relied upon as an absolute come-hell-or-high-water promise. Here too we may encounter the plea of 'you didn't understand

The Dutch managing director of an OEM company operating across Europe comments on varying reactions when quoting on projects:

"When we offer to design the customer's installation...

... if he's French, he's flattered and says 'yes'.
... if he's German, he responds cautiously,
    says 'yes but' and means 'no'.

When we offer to enhance his own design...

... if he's French, he says 'super!'
... if he's German, he says 'make a quote to my
    specification so that I can compare your price
    with the others!'

The French - and the British - like to be able to go back to the boss and say 'look, we've worked out how to do it better'. Not the Germans."

He cites the case of a German engineer who counted up the number of electric motors and conveyor rollers in a handling system in order to make a comparison with other quotes. He then complained that he was getting less motors and rollers for the same price, and was unimpressed by the argument that this meant less electricity consumption and less maintenance...

what I meant you to understand' and, if the plea for modification or total exculpation is rejected, Italians can be adept at finding ways and means to delay, defer and deter the ultimate execution of their part of what was intended by both sides to be a waterproof contract."

In contrast to the French and Italians, the **Swiss** shun any form of theatricality. By dint of their earnestness in such matters, they have earned a reputation as Europe's most exasperating negotiators, either grinding down the opposition or bringing everything to a standstill. The Belgian general manager of a US multinational even goes so far as to say that "the German Swiss are so straightforward that you don't even have to 'see through them'. You can easily guess their negotiating strategy." Even the Italian Swiss are so meticulous in their attention to detail that they drive the average Italian mad.

189

Austrians, as even the most casual observer will have remarked, are as like the Swiss as chalk and cheese. A study undertaken in 1992 by the Cranfield School of Management noted "a non-confrontational style of operation among Austrian management, a desire to agree, achieve consensus, and avoid disharmony. 'Charm' appears to be an important ingredient in the Austrian management style." An Indian businessman quoted by Norwegian authors Kjell Habert and Arild Lillebø is even more emphatic: "Austrians... do not have set rules; they see which way the wind is blowing and act accordingly."

In negotiations, the **Dutch** say what they think and expect you to do the same. They also, according to a Belgian manager, "do things by the book." All of this, on the face of it, makes it easier to do business. Yet they are known to play tricks, a habit that may have something to do with the satisfaction of outwitting a competitor.

A Belgian manager with a US multinational points out that "the Dutch will pretend they understand and agree with you even when this is not the case." A senior Dutch executive concurs - "they say 'yes' but it may mean 'no'" - but for him the judgement only refers to the people in the southernmost provinces of Limburg, Noord-Brabant and Zeeuws Vlaanderen (the 'Burgundian' bits of The Netherlands)!

Another Belgian executive (they love talking about the Dutch, and *vice versa*!) says that "when they listen to you, you feel they are thinking only in terms of reasons for not accepting your opinion." In that sense, they are not unlike the British.

Once you know this, you have the advantage in two respects. In the first place, as a Belgian IT executive remarked to me, the Dutch seem to be permanently programmed in 'teaching mode' (though, being a democratic people, they moralise as much to themselves as they do to others). This may provide the opportunity to act the good listener and play on their vanity.

The second aspect evoked by this perceptive Belgian is that the Dutch tend to focus so singlemindedly on an agreed objective that, even if they suspect there may be an alternative strategy that would serve their case better, they will stick to the appointed task. So, again, you know where you are with them.

Once the deal is clinched, it's not like the Dutch to renege. An American sales director with an OEM multinational comments that the Dutch "are tough but fair during the demonstration stage, very tough on price but, once the decision's taken, that's it."

As you may have gathered from the above, the **Belgian** negotiating manner, Flemish and Walloon, is the opposite of the Dutch. It is not their style to stick on matters of principle, although they have clear principles of their own. Their approach is more exploratory, relation-oriented and flexible. They have good listening skills, which doesn't mean they necessarily agree with you.

Where the Dutch will insist, in project work, on respecting the original specification to the finest detail, the Belgians will compromise intelligently in order to eliminate a problem. Saved by the willingness of his Belgian supplier team, a German company director commented: "You can come to some sort of compromise with the Belgians. With the Dutch it's much more difficult!"

As for the **Nordics**, the Indian businessman referred to earlier comments that "Norwegians come with preconceived notions, set on their strategies. The Swedes are more sensitive than the Norwegians and very good at negotiating." A Swede concurs: "Norwegians make decisions too hastily. They don't research seriously. They will readily make a verbal agreement. The Swedes are more thorough. They do their research, and they expect written agreements."

Elsewhere, Habert and Lillebø's book quotes the views of a Dutchman: "Personal contacts and relations with Scandinavian people are considered open, trustful and reliable. However, the Swedes are not easygoing but have a stiff, hard, businesswise attitude. In contrast, Danish people are open and friendly. We consider Norwegian people in between, which is beneficial for a good, longlasting relationship."

Speaking of the Norwegians, a French business executive says that they "very seldom openly oppose their interlocutor,

191

even when they in fact totally disagree with him. They would rather switch to a different matter in order to come back to the first one at a later stage of the negotiation."

Another observer, an American businessman, comments that "Norwegians are inclined to negotiate like they would with their grandmother, with full trust and no strategy or plans. They lay the cards on the table, face up, right away, not saving anything for possible surprises." They even have a dislike for what they view as unnecessary legal formalities and costs, prompting a German business lawyer quoted by Habert and Lillebø to say that they are "often regarded as naive and credulous."

As sensitive negotiators, the Swedes bargain hard but almost always politely. Ultimately, like the British, they prefer to avoid adversarial business relationships. Jean Phillips-Martinsson goes so far as to say that the Swede "is totally inflexible in negotiations. He doesn't negotiate at all. He says 'let's discuss my proposal', but has no intention of discussing anything, his mind is made up."

No wonder the Swedes, like most Nordics, are comfortable with silence! As Ms Phillips-Martinsson says, "they use it to digest your questions, formulate their reply and to motivate their next move..." Elsewhere she makes the interesting observation that "in Swedish eyes, being honest means telling the truth and keeping your word. This means that he is unlikely to give compliments as, in his eyes, it would be an exaggeration of the truth"!

Perhaps surprisingly, attention to detail applies to the **Greeks** as much as to the Dutch. Richard Mead makes the point that "the Greek shows good will and good faith **not** by cutting the discussion to the main points but by examining every detail. This lengthening of discussion time in order to develop the relationship signifies good manners, not the reverse as in the Anglo cultures."

... and when they 're playing tricky

Sometimes, of course, the purpose of negotiations is to catch the other side out - although this is not a very honour-able objective, nor even a very intelligent one if you want to enjoy a trusting and even-handed relationship with the other party in the future. Yet a bit of chicanery enters into most negotiations. The challenge, and the fun of the chase, get the upper hand...

Even if more than 65 per cent of all communications is non-verbal, as some experts claim, it is the spoken language that dominates and determines the outcome of negotiations, not just in terms of the ability to use a language but the **way** in which it is used. A foreigner will speak English in a much more literal way than an English-speaker, who may be tempted to manipulate the language to suit his own ends. Then there's the problem of British understatement: Jean Phillips-Martinsson comments rightly that this "is guaranteed to mislead and frustrate the Swedes [and most other Europeans] and even those whose mother-tongue is English!"

English being the *lingua franca* of so many multinational

Robert Zoellick, a GATT negotiator in the Bush administration, gave his opinion on European negotiation tactics to the *Le Figaro* daily in late-1993:

"You are confronted with two kinds of people: the 'technicians' who know the dossier but can't take decisions, and the political delegates empowered to take decisions who don't know anything. So you have to find, for every country, someone in between who is both competent and closely linked to the decision-makers.

In France, these people don't exist. I could find the right kind of people in Brussels but, in France, it was difficult. There was meeting after meeting, but no real outcome.

When you are negotiating, everything depends on trust. You have to invest time, even in a non-crisis situation, to develop relationships. With the Germans and the British, it's easy. With the French, it's difficult to estab-lish informal contacts to verify their position and thus avoid conflict.

The French system does not encourage individual initiative. I'm talking about the bureaucratic hierarchy based on the ENA... I find the French system more opaque."

---

companies, the British have an apparent natural advantage in negotiations as well as a disproportionately big impact on meetings within their own companies. The British communications manager of a major Paris-based international corporation remarks that his French colleagues often complain that they think they have agreed something with their British opposite numbers and minute it carefully, only to be told that that wasn't what was agreed. The negotiations are conducted in English, so the problem can be misunderstanding by the French, misuse of the language by the British, or maybe something else...

A Scots colleague who has frequently represented French companies in negotiations with English associates has this to say: "There is a theory that much misunderstanding arises because the number of words in the tongue of Shakespeare is far, far greater than in that of Molière. English derives from both Latin and various Germanic roots, permitting the English to express those delicate shades of meaning which permit one to interpret *post facto* and for one's own convenience what has been verbally expressed." To which one can add that, despite or maybe because of this degree of refinement, statements made in English often seem to be vaguer than their foreign-language equivalents.

The apparent language barrier can also be a useful negotiating tool. An American business executive quoted by Habert and Lillebø comments that "Norwegians use the fact that they are not talking in their own language to great effect. It gives them the opportunity to ask very direct and pointed questions without offending, because they can apologize for the question based on their language proficiencies, which are usually excellent. They also ask for clarification of a word or a statement which they understood the first time, but it gives them more time to study the reply." Cunning.

While verbal input will ultimately determine the outcome of negotiations, much depends on skilful interpretation of involuntary non-verbal signals from the other side. Unease with a situation or deliberate attempts to mislead may, though not always, be communicated through a shifting of the body, uncrossing the legs, and so on. Perfectionists will even tell you that dilation of the pupils indicates a conciliatory stance, constriction a combative one. That's why some people wear sunglasses indoors...

Much of the above applies to all cross-cultural negotiating situations, strategic or otherwise. But a few words should also be said about marketing negotiations, which represent a different scenario because of the typical status differential between the buyer and seller roles, which is more pronounced than in the case of a complex transaction like a company acquisition. A multicultural group of researchers undertook a comparative study of French, German, British and American sales negotiation techniques, the results of which were published in the April 1988 issue of the *Journal of Marketing*[40].

Essentially two types of negotiating strategy were identified. The first is the problem-solving approach (PSA), which is particularly popular with Anglo-Saxons: here, the behaviour of both parties is inclined to be "cooperative, integrative, and information-exchange-oriented", i.e. both sides, and particularly the prospective buyer, volunteer input on their needs and preferences.

The second strategy is defined as distributive bargaining, where the aim is to "change a target's attitudes, attributions, or actions. Promises and threats are examples of distributive or instrumental appeals" designed to induce concession-making by the other party.

A negotiation simulation was set up with samples of more than 40 experienced businesspeople from the countries concerned. Among the conclusions was that interpersonal attraction and similarity enhance buyer satisfaction with the French. Status and context, i.e. situational constraints, also make a difference to the outcome. "Negotiator characteristics apparently have a key role in negotiations between French businesspeople. This finding suggests that managers might consider choosing sales representatives who are similar in background and personality to their French clients." And how!

By contrast, cooperativeness or the use of the problem-solving approach (PSA) appears to be far less effective in the case of what Edward Hall calls the 'low context' Germans. Hence the use of what has been variously described as the German 'hard sell' or, in the words of Klaus Schmidt, the 'dogmatic air'. "German sellers appear to walk a tightrope in negotiations. With the dual goals of high individual profit and high buyer satisfaction, German negotiators apparently must make a tradeoff between the two."

In the case of the British, the researchers found that similarity helped, but that "status relationships determined **before** the negotiations begin have a more important influence on outcomes than does the actual process... Status or role seems to be crucial in British negotiations."

So status or role is most important to the British and least important to the Germans, with the French somewhere in between.

Le dernier mot...

"You have to start with the French at a basic, personal relationship level. Then you develop the relationship over time and in successive layers, moving more and more towards 'specifics', building trust as you progress. If you don't take this often long time to construct such a foundation for doing business, you can expect a complete lack of follow-up to a meeting or even to a written agreement like a Memo of Understanding. In the absence of a firm foundation and a lot of consensus-building, what you think was a firm agreement will have been totally 'forgotten'".

Jan Loeber, Brussels-based US CEO

"You agree the points of principle for your clients with the French in the morning, then go off precisely on the stroke of one o'clock for a five-course lunch where you talk about everything except business. You go back home thinking everything's fine, only to receive a fax the following morning saying they disagree with at least one of the points of principle. I sometimes wonder whether the French only really think when they're digesting or asleep. This has happened to me at least a dozen times."

John McBride, British management consultant, Kent

"The hardest job for any manager is to merge his firm with another"

The Economist

"I'm glad to say that we made it, that this has been a successful merger"

Pasquale Pistorio, CEO SGS-Thomson

"French, British and Dutch managers see their German counterparts as narrow-minded, inflexible and aggressive, although also fair and reliable"

Wall Street Journal Europe

"There's no question that nationalism is a major problem for a lot of European companies that need to merge or take each other over in an effort to consolidate their industries"

Constantinos Markides, London Business School

"There is a tendency to overanalyse and split hairs - spaccare il capello in quattro*"*

John Mole, speaking of the Italians

"The Americans and British apparently possess M&A skills which many of the French have yet to acquire"

The Economist

"It is far easier to buy a company than to make the acquisition work"

International Herald Tribune

THE CRUNCH POINTS

mergers & strategic alliances

We live in an age of international realignment - ratio-nalisation, mergers, joint ventures, strategic alliances - where the need to reconcile different national and corporate cultures is critical. M&A business, which almost dried up during the last recession, seems now to have become the flavour of the age...

Recent experience has taught management that there are alternatives to outright merger or acquisition, including various kinds of strategic alliance and, most anodine of all, joint ventures. However, they all contain the germs of cross-cultural conflict.

Getting different corporate **and** national cultures to integrate harmoniously is an enormous challenge. It is estimated that, even in the case of mergers between companies in the same country, 50 per cent are deemed less than satisfactory - and this is a best case scenario. In the words of *The Economist*, "those who have gone grey from the experience say that at least half of all mergers fail to meet their objectives."

Business consultants say that, of all the things that can go wrong when two or more companies decide to live together, the most telling factor is cultural incompatibility, a matter of human chemistry. British corporate psychologist Paul Thorne offers the following advice: "When initiating a merger, one of the most important things you can do is to encourage the other company to expose and explain its culture. Then examine and systematise its value system."

This does not just imply a clash of national cultures, jump-started by the linguistic problems (the single most important decision in such situations is to agree, at least, on a common language - not always an easy achievement!). The issue is far more complicated, with a number of parallel factors overlapping and intertwining. Intimately linked with the national cultures, however nuanced these may be, are different corporate and even professional cultures.

These in turn may be independent of, but influenced by, the precise management styles of the people currently in charge on both sides. Everything is further complicated by differences in the structural-hierarchical organisation of the companies concerned, the decision-making processes, the reporting procedures and so on - not to mention the psychological impact on employees of the whole process, plus external industry and contractual constraints.

The only safe way to meet such challenges is by auditing all aspects thoroughly and regularly on all sites, since cultures can vary by location even within a single country. Employee opinions and perceptions should be treated in confidence. Senior managers on both sides need to be bought into the process and groomed individually to represent the new organisation's policies and philosophies.

Reflecting the 'grassroots' origins of so many small businesses, the SME sector demonstrates particular reluctance to come out into the open. On the contrary, the most common response associated with the prospect of greater cross-border activity is the NIMBY (Not-In-My-Back-Yard) syndrome. So the question of cross-cultural teamwork rarely arises

Even the German *Mittelstand* - along with British small-to-medium business, the most outward-looking SME sector of the larger trading nations - is reluctant to enter into relationships outside its normal stamping grounds. A study by DG XXIII of the European Commission in June 1992 found that German companies prefer to work with fellow-SMEs in northern and central Europe, and hesitate to enter into relationships with partners further south.

Such hesitancies must distress Eurocrats and others who are trying to instill a greater sense of entrepreneurship in SMEs, rated as the white hope of Europe in terms of future growth and job creation. Much may have to await the emergence of new generations of managers, better educated in both general and professional terms. Fortunately, business schools are starting specifically to address the issue of entrepreneurship: British institutions are in the lead, followed by the Scandinavians.

The experience of the Dutch Philips group buying into the German Grundig company is a classic example of cultural incompatibility. Differences in the corporate cultures of the two firms were exacerbated by differences in national cultures. The biggest hurdle was the bureaucratic mentality of the Grundig hierarchy (as much a reflection of the national culture as a corporate culture in its own right), which drove even the methodical Dutch to despair. Philips has now resolved the issue first by buying a controlling interest in the German company and, secondly, reorganising Grundig into a dozen product divisions.

Other cases of failed international mergers include Unidata, a half-hearted effort to create a European computer industry, Hoesch-Hoogovens, Dunlop-Pirelli and a lot that are less well known.

Apart from the human chemistry aspect, the international M&A process can run up against very precise technico-cultural issues right at the outset. The Anglo-Saxon style of hostile takeover is still alien to most continental European business cultures, partly because defence mechanisms make it ineffectual: German corporations use their banks to block takeovers with proxy votes, while in other countries majorities are in family hands. And where continental bids **are** hostile, they tend by comparison to be less transparent.

When it comes to committing things to paper, Anglo-Saxon corporate lawyers are astonished to find that French companies are often bought and sold on simple contracts devoid of the representations and warranties, conditions of closing and other forms of legal protection they consider normal.

Indeed national legal systems, still a long way from being harmonised within the European Union, cast long shadows across international mergers. René Olie of the University of Limburg's department of economics and business administration gives the example of a German-Dutch initiative: "In one case of a failed merger the new international corporation, on the advice of a famous consultancy firm, introduced a product-based divisional structure. This new structure cut right across the legal structure of the corporation, which still followed national lines. It turned out that the Dutch were able to work within this setup; the Germans were not."

European Management Style

Leading from the Front

Such a group is typified by executives from the United Kingdom, Spain and, to a lesser degree, Ireland. They can be described as 'autocratic' with 'strong drive'. They are also 'people oriented' in that they like to show strong leadership qualities and would work towards forming strategies that would be in the organisation's interests. However, the rest of the organisation has to fit with their approach and style.

Towards a Common Goal

This grouping consists of executives who are professional, who display strong drive with effective follow-through. They are likely to be disciplined and state that the systems, controls and procedures within the organisation are not a hindrance to job performance. The majority of German and Austrian executives fit into this classification. Efficiency and goal attainment are the prime motivators of executives in this group.

Managing from a Distance

The majority of French executives in the sample tend to display autocracy and drive, but manage from a distance. They are identified as being strategic/conceptual thinkers and understand a need for procedures, but are likely to lack discipline in implementation. For example, they could generate resentment among subordinates because they may not be communicating messages or objectives effectively.

Consensus

The members of this group are very much team-oriented. Senior executives from Sweden, Finland and, to a certain extent, Ireland are more likely to fall into this category. It goes someway to explaining why a vision is more likely to be shared by executives in the

Scandinavian countries... Such executives place emphasis on people, effective communication and on attention to detail. The research shows that, if a senior executive in this grouping was not paying attention to people and was not communicating effectively, then team performance would be significantly impaired.

•••

The data shows that one style of operation could have a serious impact on the way another style operates. This can have negative effects on the business. The formation of the multinational team will therefore require careful planning to make sure that the right blend of management styles are represented on that team. Both leaders and members of the team need to be aware of the differing individual and team styles operating throughout the European context to enable the identification of potential areas of conflict and to anticipate and deal with them as and when they arise. The success of a multinational team depends on such sensitivities and insights.

The Cranfield Executive Competencies Survey:
Professor Andrew Kakabadse

There are other obstacles in the path of would-be raiders. In terms of valid financial information Dutch companies, like their German neighbours, tend to give very little away to the outsider. There are now 800,000 *b.v.'s*, with their limited information filing requirements, compared with only 5,000 *n.v.'s*, which require full disclosure.

These mechanistic aspects of merger and management - which frequently find their origins in national cultures - have to be brought into line to achieve total integration. No wonder so many international corporate marriages ultimately come apart.

I could cite a series of such experiences over the last 20 years. One of the earliest was the Dunlop-Pirelli venture, a disaster for various reasons. Another precocious attempt was Agfa-Gevaert, a Belgo-German alliance where the German parent, Bayer, bought complete control ten years on as the only way out of its problems. André Leysen, who managed the Belgian side of the operation, later commented to the press that "an equal-status agreement between two nationalities almost never works. There must be one boss."

Even this didn't resolve the issue in the case of what was described at the time as "the model pan-European firm" and "the first of a new, European breed of company." CarnaudMetalbox (CMB) was the product of a merger between the French Carnaud company and Britain's Metalbox Packaging, two widely differing corporate cultures. Jean-Marie Descarpentries, Carnaud's boss at the time, continued to run the merged venture in his distinctive and in some respects distinctly Gallic way - what the British side saw, according to *The Wall Street Journal Europe*, as a "maverick, interventionist management style that left little room for the input of others." Metalbox alumni, the *WSJE* added, "tended to seek order and coordination, while he actively sought creative confusion."

Since then an innocent American company, Whirlpool International, has been dragged into the European N-I-H (Not Invented Here) arena on acquiring control of its joint venture with the Dutch Philips organisation. In the words of *The Economist* it inherited a situation where "bitter rivalry between the employees of Bauknecht, a fiercely independent German company, and those of Philips, which took over Bauknecht in 1984, had soured the atmosphere within the firm."

Yet another example of 'post-alliance culture shock' is the case, cited by Marc Raynaud of Inter Cultural Management Associates, of a US-owned Swedish group acquired by a young and entrepreneurial French company. To quote Raynaud's words: "The Swedes quickly perceived the French management as hierarchical [yes, even in a young and entrepreneurial company!] and somewhat arrogant. The French, for their part, were exasperated by what they saw as the naive, cautious, weakwilled behaviour of the Swedes."

206

Perception, of course, depends on where you're coming from. Interviewed for the *Harvard Business Review* book 'Leaders on Leadership' in 1992, Swedish top manager Percy Barnevik turned the tables - but in this case on the Swiss: "a Swede may think a Swiss is not completely frank and open, that he doesn't know where he stands. Swiss culture shuns disagreement. A Swiss might say, 'Let's come back to that point later, let me review it with my colleagues'. A Swede would prefer to confront the issue directly."

As the man who engineered the merger of the Swedish ASEA and the Swiss Brown Boveri companies, Barnevik knew what he was talking about. In fact, it is significant that mergers of firms originating in less ethnocentric countries seem to work relatively well. ABB, formed in 1988, is the prime example. Swedish industry used to practise a form of management colonialism by sending nationals on tours of duty which did little to encourage continuity and employee identity. Now ABB spurns expatriates for local people who speak English and "think globally" (see page 251).

One of the solutions, an admirably cautious one, is to approach the marriage of two organisations through an intermediate 'engagement' period - for example by mounting a joint venture before attempting a merger. This has worked well for the Alstom organisation, one of ABB's main competitors in international markets. The two parties involved, the French Alcatel Alsthom and the British General Electric Co, first established a 50/50 joint venture registered in The Netherlands as GEC Alsthom NV. In mid-1998 this extremely successful joint-venture partnership took the plunge to emerge as a company in its own right. The two parents have retained a major interest in Alstom (note the spelling!) while allowing it now to run as an independent business.

Nothing venture...

Two incidents in a British-Belgian joint venture in the petrochemical industry illustrate the impact of national cultures on professional behaviour:

1. *Technical standards*: Application of the agreed plant specification differed. The Belgian partner stuck rigidly to the specification, the British partner came up with a series of options designed to provide a comparable, or superior, solution at less cost. The Belgian partner refused to consider any of these options.

Moral: The British partner welcomed a challenge to its creativity, the Belgian partner 'did it by the book'.

2. *Safety standards*: The installation represented a potential safety risk to the community where the plant was sited. Both parties acknowledged the need for safety measures. The Belgian partner addressed the relevant legislation - and then fudged it. The British partner, after examining the issues involved, proposed measures exceeding the legal minima.

Moral: The Belgian partner pretended to observe the letter of the law, the British partner respected the spirit of the law.

"The Germans say 'that's not possible here because of the law' when the first thought of the French and the Belgians is 'that's the law, how can we get around it?'"

Belgian company director

"The French are both challenging and charming to work with. They expect you, at one and the same time, to use your imagination and to establish a personal relationship"

Swedish international marketing director

"Some would say that Spaniards work poorly in teams"

Helen Wattley Ames, *Spain is Different*

"The Dutch are motivated to be innovative and creative out of concern for economy and functionality. The French are creative out of sheer enjoyment. The British are just naturally creative"

Belgian architect

"My experience is that the Spanish work increasingly well in teams, particularly multi-cultural ones. They are discreet, yet don't hesitate to state their position. They're excellent management material"

American multinational CEO

"The French, when they talk, they feel they are growing"

Belgian human resources director

"Italian business relationships are based on mutual dependence and a sense of mutual obligation most easily satisfied with members of the extended family"

John Mole, *Mind your Manners*

"The Italians will always tell you you can't do it here (in Italy). The Dutch will tell you you can't do it anywhere."

American multinational CEO

"None of us is as smart as all of us"

Kenneth Blanchard

THE CRUNCH POINTS

multicultural teamwork

The potential for cross-cultural synergy in international project teams is enormous. Management writer Tom Lester takes the example of an Anglo-French joint venture: "French conceptual grandeur can make a potent force if wedded to British pragmatism as at GEC-Alsthom, equally successful in high-speed trains and generating equipment." Today's Alstom (see page 207) is the result.

Good examples of multicultural teams include the joint Anglo-Italian EVC chemicals venture, where British and Italian MDs alternate every five years; the Swedish-Swiss ABB group using the 'Think Global, Act Local' approach; and the Finnish Kone organisation, which has shown exceptional sensitivity in developing an international presence. Jean Phillips-Martinsson also makes the intriguing point that Swedish multinationals frequently employ Italians to manage their subsidiaries around the world!

The challenge in multicultural teamwork is of course to achieve the required level of synergy in the first place. A lot of the initial difficulties can in fact be attributed to linguistics. The French expect foreign nationals to speak their language like Gallics to the manner born, yet they are prone themselves to making extravagant statements in English, with surprising results. When a French group sent its newly acquired UK subsidiary a fax with the words "we demand your latest profit figures", they may actually have meant it. French management is like that.

At the same time, in defence of French management - and here they depart from the official governmental line - they do accept the reality of English as the *lingua franca* of business. The top brass in enlightened multinationals like Alcatel and Schlumberger are all insistent that multicultural meetings within their companies be held in what, for them, is a foreign tongue (which doesn't prevent Alcatel from giving nearly all its important corporate jobs to graduates of the *Grandes Ecoles*). Imagine British multinationals **imposing** the use of French on their divisions serving French Africa! A firm line on language is a prerequisite for a multicultural team of any size.

Creating an effective team also means recognising at the outset that differences in value systems and priorities exist

213

between the European trading cultures. Even if one can make good an educational deficiency in a potential all-rounder's knowhow and skills, there are still some almost Freudian predispositions which have to be taken into account. Although changes are evident in the younger generation, it is true to say that many French executives still have an aversion to risk-taking or even taking a personal initiative.

While the British often manage to reconcile individual ambition with a natural flair for teamwork, as many international managers and academics have noted, the French tend to find teamwork difficult. As John Mole says in his book *Mind your Manners*: "In business, competitiveness [between French colleagues] is fostered by strong vertical hierarchies. Far from refreshing, people find it disconcerting when others do not compete. They will not wait for a group consensus before taking an initiative. To those from more participative cultures this can appear deliberately provocative. Foreigners used to a team approach will usually have to adjust their expectations of working relationships."

Essentially, self-respecting French executives are thought- rather than action-oriented. A Parisian lawyer makes the point with typically and disarmingly brutal frankness: "French managers perceive their work as an intellectual challenge, requiring only application of individual brainpower. They abhor action and favour intellectual endeavour, as all that matters is the ability to demonstrate one's ability to grasp complex issues, analyse problems, manipulate ideas and evaluate solutions."

This, together with a natural reluctance to play second fiddle (a normal stance in a sales situation), may explain why, in the words of researcher Klaus Schmidt, "the French have not traditionally held selling in high esteem." They tend to have a distaste for sales, customer service and related activities that make demands on their egos. The same is also evident to a lesser degree in the Spanish.

An American businessman running his hi-tech company's French sales subsidiary commented to the *International Herald Tribune* that, despite "drilling, drilling, drilling", his employees still forget that they should not argue with customers, that they should try to be of service, and that they should make a point of returning phonecalls.

A Danish marketing VP confirms the problem: "I have great difficulty getting my French salespeople to look at things from the customer's point of view. If they get into an argument with him out of conviction that their vision of things is the right one, then the customer's wrong! Period."

The same tendency is evident in the Spanish, though they are less likely to argue. Helen Wattley Ames makes the point that Spaniards "are quite likely, especially in a group, to keep quiet when someone says something they don't agree with. There are reasons for this: fear of repercussions if the person is a superior or suspicion if someone is not well known." Direct confrontation is also considered impolite.

Yet, in a multicultural context, Spaniards can shine when properly motivated: "At conferences where both Spaniards and foreigners are giving presentations, it is interesting to see how many of the Spanish presentations are the work of a team, while the other presentations are usually the work of individuals." But John Mole makes the point that "the concept of a team, if it exists at all, is one of individuals working independently under a strong leader."

Germans face a different challenge when integrating with multicultural teams, their problem being that they come from a society which worships the cult of specialisation - something that by definition runs counter to the principle of shared decisions. However, given a bit of the sense of application for which they are justly famous, they turn into highly competent and cooperative team members.

In this respect, they rate with the British and the representatives of the smaller countries of Europe, the Benelux and Nordic ones. The British, when they get the better of their Britishness, are extremely good team members once they know which side they're on. The people of the Benelux and Nordic countries, with their less ethnocentric cultures, are even better disposed to working in a pluralist and multicultural environment.

Yet even here there can be problems. The Dutch, according to one foreign observer, have difficulty in thinking strat-

215

The professional challenge

In researching for this book I discovered that, in some multinational organisations, professional cultures starkly override national ones. One example was a consumer foods company where the engineers - culturally a very motley lot - stood in serried ranks facing off the marketers. Other companies ranged the commercial people up against the accountants. I even had one Swedish bean-counter who absolutely insisted on my reducing my observational approach to a classic Four-Square model. I refused to do so.

The only constructive outcome of this was a joke told me, as will be evident, by the engineers. It concerns a businessman on safari who runs into a headhunter (the real kind, not an executive search consultant) who is selling human brains by the kilo. The businessman is intrigued by the fact that engineers' and accountants' brains are selling at $10 per kilo, while marketers' brains are priced at $20 per kilo. He asks the head-hunter why this is. "To get a kilo of marketers' brains, I have to kill twice as many", the headhunter replies.

egically: they are so down-to-earth that they can only take abstract concepts on board with difficulty, they have to have them spelled out. "As a pragmatic people, the Dutch are unhappy with a high level of abstraction", he says. They can also be very resistant to people who they feel are playing too much on their charisma, a very unDutch characteristic: they may make allowances for the extrovert behaviour of the Mediterraneans, but British or French expansiveness may be greeted rather coldly.

Conventional wisdom would suggest that the experience of working in a multicultural environment, for example as an executive in a multinational corporation, would *per se* help to defuse such issues. Not so, it seems. Geert Hofstede believes that long periods of formal training may actually reinforce cultural predispositions rather than attenuate them.

216

André Laurent concluded from studies undertaken at INSEAD that working in a multicultural environment could heighten the contrasts in management ideologies, "with fairly differentiated images of organisations and their management". Northern Europeans, he maintained, tend to define organisation in terms of functions, while southern Europeans see organisation more in terms of social status and authority.

It seems that this may not be a drawback. Talking to *The European* newspaper Mac Bolton, assistant director of the Roffey Park Management Institute in the UK, commented: "There is a pattern of expectations of what people are like. If someone does not match up to these expectations, people get a bit puzzled. The trick is to retain some of the characteristics that people expect, while being very open to people who are different and respecting their differences."

Business being what it is, there is always room for friction in every team, multi- or mono-cultural. Commenting on the conclusions of his Cranfield Executive Competencies Survey, Professor Kakabadse says: "The strategic concerns of top management in mid- to large-sized European corporate organisations are shared, irrespective of nationality. In effect, differences and acrimony are a natural part of the process of addressing difficult and complex issues. The difference between a mediocre and a more effective business organisation is **not** the lack of tension but a concentrated effort to ensure for a high-quality dialogue. The challenge for top management is how to address sensitive issues, such as reconciling strategic options and negotiating to improve the quality of relationships and dialogue amongst the members of the Senior Executive. Are German management any better than the French or the British? - all are in the same boat."

Further on, he comments: "The essential finding from the Cranfield survey is that teams are vital... the prime mechanism for the consideration and implementation of policies and strategies." And a bit further on: "Turning a top-level management group into a high-performing top team is not based on providing additional insights, i.e. giving more information such as consultancy reports, but more on **actioning the insights** that exist within the group. Whether British, Irish, German, French or Spanish, the actioning insight process is common to all nationalities - get people to talk to each other, tease out the sensitivities, but as comfortably as possible so that the level of disruption does not become destructive..."

Various research studies have consistently shown that, in 90 per cent of cases, groups are more successful in problem-solving than individuals. The same research has shown that, if these teams happen to be multicultural ones, then the insights can be even richer...

"Organisational methods based on decentralisation, target setting and functional specialisation are fast taking root creating a serious generation gap between younger and older managers over 50"

John Mole, speaking of Spanish management

"In business reengineering, old job titles and old organizational arrangements - departments, divisions, groups, and so on - cease to matter. They are artifacts of another age... Reengineering capitalizes on the same characteristics that have traditionally made Americans such great business innovators: individualism, self-reliance, a willingness to accept risk, and a propensity for change"

Michael Hammer and James Champy,
Reengineering the Corporation

"A new factor, that of rapid change, has come into the world. We have not yet learned how to adjust ourselves to its economic and social consequencies"

Wallace B Donham, <u>1932</u>

"Ours is a transition period. What the future society will look like, let alone whether it will indeed be the 'knowledge society' some of us dare hope for, depends on how the developed countries respond to the challenges of this transition period"

Peter Drucker, 1993

It is true that in his sanctum sanctorum *– that secret place of his heart where he keeps his most sacred prejudices – the reader may treasure the unavowed belief that an American is superior to an Italian. He is entitled to his prejudice. And I respect it. I even think it may be useful in order to counterbalance the prejudice which the Italian no doubt treasures to the effect that he is superior to the American. All that kind of thing keeps the world going and there is not too much harm in it, provided prejudices – like dogs – are trained to behave.*

Salvador de Madariaga, *Americans*

THE CRUNCH POINTS

'New Age' organisation and change

In the opening chapter of this book I stated that, of the five dimensions identified by Geert Hofstede, I found uncertainty avoidance to be the most revealing. Individualism/collectivism, masculinity/femininity and short-term/long-term orientation offer nuances but few surprises, while power distance is both easily recognisable where it still prevails and susceptible to erosion in the long term by the democratisation of society and business.

Uncertainty avoidance, on the other hand, leads us into positively Freudian depths. For a long time to come it will continue to haunt some European cultures more than others. It therefore deserves closer examination in its own right.

There is an additional and very urgent reason for giving it due attention, namely the element of **change**. European business cultures have evolved in a relatively stable environment where corporate structures and decision-making processes are based on certain assumptions: consumer expectations, market demands, economic trends.

This is now no longer the case, and the mayhem this climate of change inflicts on many strong uncertainty avoidance cultures is enormous. Those with high creativity potential, like France, fare better than a culture like Germany, where uncertainty avoidance is closely linked with conservatism.

Peter Drucker directed the following typically oracular message to a management audience in 1992: "There will be no strong governments in the west for the next ten years. So you will have to be able to do business in an unstable political situation, where no government is going to be able to govern effectively. Therefore, you need a feel for the major directions and fundamental trends in a very chaotic situation; so you must look to the outside and prepare yourself before you prepare your people."

In his book, *Age of Paradox*[41] Charles Handy says that "instead of being a castle, a home for life for its defenders, an organization will be more like an apartment block, an association of temporary residents gathered together for mutual convenience."

Clearly such messages will be more easily digested and assimilated by people from weak uncertainty avoidance cultures. For the strong UA folk, it can only spell discomfort. That, from Hofstede's results and my own observations, means particularly the French, the Germans, the Belgians, the Spanish, the Italians, the Austrians and the Greeks. The Swedes, the Danes and the British, if they get their act together, should make the transition relatively unscathed.

As always, it tends to be the Anglo-Saxon management experts who are most productive in coming up with panaceas (echoes of the patent medicine men of the Wild West). The irony of it is that they are offering prescriptions which may be fine for their own weak uncertainty avoidance cultures, but are as unacceptable to strong UA cultures as the change that prompts them. Far from relieving stress, they are introducing yet **another** element of uncertainty into the situation.

In some cases, France in particular, there is a resistance to Anglo-Saxon management theories *per se*. The very real cultural problems are magnified by both French dislike for what they see as over-simplification and their earnest desire to see themselves as different.

Barsoux and Lawrence tackle this problem head on in their book, published in 1990. "The current obsession with American gurus and the 'go-getting' spirit is so powerful that it would be foolhardy to criticize it out loud. Yet in private conversations, a number of managers speculated that the cult of managerialism and the public interest in management were a flash in the pan (*un phénomène de mode*) and fully expected values to go round full circle. They were simply waiting for the whole thing to blow over and for 'normal service' to be resumed... One is reminded of the way the French embraced management by objectives or quality circles in theory, but have failed to implement them successfully."

Speaking of large power distance countries in his book *Cultures and Organizations*, Geert Hofstede asserts that "packaged leadership methods invented in the USA, like management by objectives (MBO), will not work because they presuppose some form of negotiation between subordinate and superior which neither party will feel comfortable with."

The resistance of the French to packaged methods was even evident, as Barsoux and Lawrence point out, in the "relative flop of Kenneth Blanchard's *One Minute Manager* in France", where the prescription of informality and what looked like manipulative techniques ran up against French formality and the inviolability of the person.

Two prominent lines of thought are now fashionable in Anglo-Saxon management circles: first, 'downsizing' as preached by Tom Peters and, second, the concept of reengineering as popularised through the book *Reengineering the Corporation* by Michael Hammer and James Champy[42].

The move to flatter and more democratic organisations, as advocated by Tom Peters, is inimical to people of a strong UA disposition, not only because they are resistant to change, but also because they are not necessarily enamoured with the idea of personal 'empowerment', to use another fashionable Anglo-Saxon management word. Empowering them will be a dubious privilege because it implies more responsibility which, in turn, means more exposure to uncertainty.

"Peters' suggestions of cutting levels of management or even turning the organizational pyramid upside down to shift the authority to the employees who directly serve the customer represent equally alien approaches to management in the Latin and Mediterranean countries", comments Michael Hoppe.

As for reengineering, this preaches the principle of radically rethinking what a business does and how it does it. Quite rightly, it challenges the *status quo*, slaughtering sacred cows and asking people to question all the assumptions that drive their business. In short, they are inviting managers to leave their prejudices and privileges behind them, go back to the drawing board, and open the doors wide to uncertainty. Nothing could be less palatable to a strong uncertainty avoidance culture!

As the country that produced the memorable comment "our firm has been functionally organized for 95 years", Germany may look like a dubious candidate for reengineering. Specialisation and sequential (rather than lateral) thinking are dominant features of the German business mind. "It may seem a radical idea to German business and may need some adjustment in application", comments James Champy, "but with the changing fortunes of German industry, it is just as imperative there and needs to be taken aboard rapidly."

225

With increasing emphasis on the human element in securing international success, Anglo-Saxon management experts are questioning and verifying the universality of application of their techniques.

Management by Objectives (MBO)

Being by definition more a task- and performance-oriented than a relation-oriented technique, Management by Objectives has had its cultural ups and downs, the greatest resistance coming from what Edward Hall calls the 'High Context' countries of the Mediterranean (see Chapter 2).

There are other nuances too as John Humble, a British pioneer of MBO, explains: "The principles of Management by Objectives apply anywhere - they just make sense. Where there can be a problem is at the appraisal stage, where one has to nuance things depending on the culture."

"In Europe, the thing I noticed in particular was that Germans were resistant until the MBO concept was presented to them in diagrammatic form. So I came up with the *Humble-MBO-Modell*: the same things were said, but they were said with the supporting authority of a formal, mechanistic model."

"The French were more personal in orientation. At the time, in the late-'60s and early-'70s, they put the emphasis on participation with, of course, the *Humble-MBO-Modèle* in support, but in a less emphatic way than the Germans."

"In fact, everyone adapted MBO to fit their management style. That's human nature!"

Personal Benchmarking

The practical application of Management by Objectives poses further problems. Some people, particularly Mediterraneans, are allergic to the idea of having to examine their performance in the presence of superiors (let alone subordinates, as is now the case in some Anglo-Saxon organisations!). It is a challenge to their self-esteem.

Moreover to the Spanish in particular personal benchmarking introduces an unwanted competitive spirit to the gracious and collegiate atmosphere of business life. In the words of Helen Wattley Ames[25]: "Competitiveness, in particular, is associated with *envidia*, 'the Spanish vice'."

The Dutch ex-manager of a major US multinational witnessed Spanish reluctance when introducing an MBO system to his company's subsidiaries. "I found the biggest problem was with the Spanish. It wasn't even a question of management style, just human dignity. No self-respecting Spanish male is going to accept that he is average! So the results of MBO appraisals were consistently out of line with the rest of Europe. We rated people on a 1-5 scale - and 3 was positively satisfactory. But the Spaniards were always 4+, as a matter of principle. It was mutual" - superiors and subordinates conspired together - "but the rest of us at the European HQ learned how to factor this into the overall results."

"The French", he adds, "couldn't take MBO very seriously. As for the Belgians, you could say what you like, but they just didn't react."

Hardly surprising in cultures which have a fundamentally different approach to organisational life - described by someone as 'Management by *Subjectives* (MBS)'!

Matrix Management

Strong uncertainty avoidance cultures thrive on clear commands and strong leadership. Matrix management introduces an element of uncertainty. Who tells me what to do and in what circumstances? If priorities conflict, who decides? So strong UA cultures fervently believe in the words of St Matthew: "No man can serve two masters."

This is borne out convincingly by reactions to a statement posed in Michael Hoppe's study (see Chapter 2): "An organizational structure in which certain subordinates have two direct bosses should be avoided at all costs." Italy, France and Belgium, all strong UA countries, agreed with the statement. Sweden and the Netherlands did not.

And what about more traditionalist and hierarchical cultures - particularly the Latin ones of Europe - where people are, on the one hand, by instinct more relation-oriented than task-oriented and, on the other, more fearful of taking on responsibility and working in an unstructured environment? Both Management by Objectives and matrix management met resistance when they headed south through Europe (see box). Spaniards interviewed by Helen Wattley Ames concurred that, while they all felt that the book *In Search Of Excellence* was interesting, "its ideas could not be transferred indiscriminately to Spain."

A Finnish senior executive with responsibility for the European business of a major US multinational speaks from his personal experience: "Being more relation-oriented, Latins tend to need particular attention and reassurance during a process of change. I have people who just need the personal contact to feel comfortable. So much depends on the awareness and skills of managers in making sure these things are spotted in time. We have had cases where we have been alerted to an underlying problem only when a serious human resources issue has arisen. This applies especially to the Latin cultures."

Some people will even argue that European business has lost the knack of planning long-term - a charge that is normally levelled against US corporations. They suggest the typical interpretation of strategic planning is a series of incremental changes focused on where the company wants to be in six months time! Not the ideal spirit for launching into a process of fundamental adjustment, which requires both patience and strong nerves.

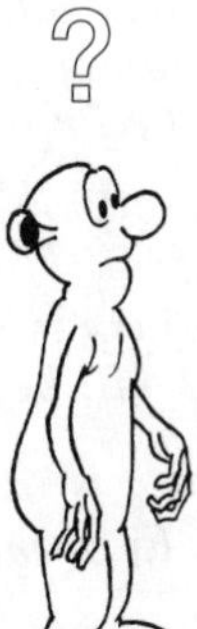

"There is a drama of cultural monotheism. All European countries have developed more or less oligarchical systems of management. These will have to adapt or face dissolution"

Jean-Fridiric Mognetti

"What you will need is an in-depth understanding of international affairs and a good interpreter to help you communicate with the aliens"

British businessman

"I think that in Europe there are no true Europeans, apart from a few over-enthusiastic expatriate Americans"

Beppe Severgnini

"What European business really needs is people who are culturally adaptable and open. You don't get that by watching language videos in your lunch hour"

Carmen Rodriguez, President, Sirecox

"In Europe's new single market the search is on for 'Euro-managers' who can work as smoothly with Germans as with Greeks"

The Economist

"Everybody is difficult in their own way. There are no saints..."

Executive search consultant

"I once wrote that in order to reach for the truth the Germans add, the French subtract and the English change the subject. I did not include the Americans, since they often give the impression that they already have the truth"

Peter Ustinov

"The jury is still out on the question of how many Euro-managers will be needed"

Executive search consultant

"The Euro-manager does not exist"

Claude Rameau, INSEAD

Chapter 6

The EuroManager

It seems that many of the world's management academics, those mentioned in this book excepted, are driven by a daemon telling them to reduce all human behaviour to a simple model. The favourite solution is the 2x2 matrix or quadrant, reflecting what Paul Thorne, a British corporate psychologist, dubs the 'Four Square Mentality'. Each square is invested by a mindset bearing the name of an animal, a god, or something else.

Paul Thorne has a typically British, pragmatic attitude: "The history of management modelling is dominated by over-simplification. A European Management Model must include models of managing, of organisation and of Europeanism. Each of these is a hugely complex reality... their inter-relationships can add confusion to confusion." I share his feelings.

If you have read this far, you will appreciate that the differences between neighbouring countries are large enough to defy such cavalier treatment. A model is a two-dimensional, sometimes a multi-dimensional, definition. Samuel Butler said that even a simple definition is "the enclosing of the wilderness of an idea within a wall of words". And here we are talking about wildernesses...

Apart from the fact that they do not have universal validity even within Europe, structured or modelled solutions are largely irrelevant in the new world economic (dis)order. It is even trite to insist that the *leitmotif* of corporate life today is change and little else.

Even before the sea-change in world business demolished a lot of theories in the mid-80s, corporate weariness with the simplistic totems of management gurus had already set in. So many names and paradigms have come and gone. The lie has also been given to the US as the shrine of management wisdom, not just through the emergence of Japan and 'The Tigers', but also through the relatively poor performance of many US corporations on the ground in Europe.

Success has often been attributed by missionary management to business philosophy or corporate ethos when, in fact, companies have been trading essentially on a superior product or service. Ample evidence of this mentality came from the proliferation of relatively meaningless corporate mission statements. But now the power of such cultures is menaced by the loss of employee loyalty caused by a process known variously as delayering, downsizing, restructuring and rationalisation.

It seems to me that only management 'philosophers' like Peter Drucker have emerged from this turmoil unscathed - people who put the emphasis on flexibility of outlook, intuition and the maximisation of human potential. The trend is toward people-oriented, rather than task-oriented, thinking. As we move towards more open markets and more global organisations, the subtleties of people management and motivation will be increasingly multifaceted and multicultural.

EuroManagers and EuroLeaders

First we have the dubious task of defining an invented word. Wherever and however the term 'EuroManager' originated, it is used promiscuously. One interpretation would have it that the word refers exclusively to a rarefied species of top executive fulfilling the role of moderator or facilitator of a multicultural team: for clarity I will henceforth refer to this paragon as a EuroLeader. According to one executive search consultant, there are probably only 2,000 jobs in Europe at present which fit this bill.

The second interpretation is that anyone with managerial responsibilities in a multicultural organisation should be a 'EuroManager': where I use the term, it will be in this sense.

A common challenge faces those involved in grooming people with potential for either of these roles: both types of job call, in the first instance, for untypical human skills. A 1993 study by Assessment Circle Europe (ACE) found that the most important qualities in would-be EuroManagers, in addition to language ability, were communication and social skills, listening skills, a sociable personality and the ability to work in a team. But, in addition, "successful EuroManagers also need to develop initiative, independence and strong planning skills in order to foresee problems and come up with creative solutions."

This combination of qualities is not going to be easy to find. At first sight, the largest European reservoir of people

234

with proven management skills is in those countries which happen to have the strongest and most hermetic cultures: France, Britain and Germany in particular. These people are *prima facie* the least naturally adapted to operating in a multicultural environment.

Their culture is to them as water is to a fish, namely something utterly essential to their existence yet something of which they are totally unaware. And the problem is that, to understand other cultures, you first have to be aware of your own. It is significant that, apart from greater facility with languages, people from the less ethnocentric (the word should really be 'culturocentric') societies of Europe are the most readily adaptable to a multicultural environment.

However, the change in perception of people from the more culturocentric societies is often considerable, once they have spent time living and working abroad. A German business academic makes the point that some of the best managers from his country are those who have managed a small foreign subsidiary: in their case it has the double advantage of both giving them cultural exposure and extending their experience into domains outside their normal specialist areas of activity.

In the same vein a British business executive remarks that the French recognise their own foibles much more readily when they have spent some time outside France. The almost defensive urge to take oneself seriously is diminished.

Another issue facing multinational management is the question of mobility. Emile Gouiran, a French lawyer, comments that "the French managerial model may have problems in the new global environment. Graduates of the *grandes écoles* have resisted moving outside France because their credentials (albeit remarkable) do not incite automatic admiration abroad. They would also have to consort with those they consider their intellectual inferiors."

In many people's minds, mobility is tantamount to insecurity - put the other way round, immobility is an apparent guarantee of security. The easiest, though not necessarily the safest, way to secure your future is to stay put. It also has the advantage that you can continue to nurture your contacts as a member of an in-group. Every European culture has a

235

Examples of how others do it - No 1

AspenTech: one 'multicultural' rule!

AspenTech is an example of a new generation of mini-multinationals. Established in 1981 to commercialise technology developed at the Massachusetts Institute of Technology (MIT), this privately held company has since become No 1 supplier of computer-based modelling and automation systems to the world's process industries. In addition to its US and Asian operations AspenTech, which employs 1,500 people, has subsidiaries in eleven European locations with a headcount of 350.

Ken Morse - now a consultant with AspenTech Europe and operating out of Cambridge (MA), where he heads the MIT's Entrepreneurship Center - started the European operation within five months of the company's formation. Jumping in at the deep end by tackling the French chemicals industry on its own ground, AspenTech Europe broke into two key accounts and then set off on the conquest of the rest of the continent. Growth has since averaged more than 30 per cent per annum and the European head office, based in Brussels, now fields a team of more than 40 people of eight different nationalities.

"What we were building was an international team that was focused on the customer", says Morse. "Our market competence meant that we sold more effectively, we also attracted attention - a number of European companies have since elected to join forces with us - and we developed a multicultural team that was naturally self-motivating because everyone shared in the fun and the success."

AspenTech Europe, now headed by German Horst Michael Böttcher, has one multicultural rule on recruitment and that is that candidates **must** speak more than one language. Otherwise the company prefers to have Italians selling and supporting in Italy, and so on. The fact that its clients include the largest firms in the process industries means it can afford to invest in people in this way. AspenTech considers its future lies in cloning subsidiary operations at country level - by continuously moving its people closer to the customer, it is also solving the problems of growth.

The multicultural challenge facing AspenTech, both inside and outside the organisation, has in fact been mitigated by some factors which also favour other mini-multis of this class: a 'niche' market where technical excellence sells, and a strong disciplinary culture rooted in chemical engineering. The company also has the advantage of being manageable in size, with the chief executive rubbing shoulders regularly with the other members of the team.

AspenTech Europe executives are a youthful bunch, which may help explain their cross-cultural harmony and their 'work hard, play hard' camaraderie. By keeping units to human dimensions, the company is maximising personal relations and the team spirit, and keeping the potential for cultural conflict to a minimum.

series of 'clubs' at its core and, rather than loosening their grip on the business world, they seem to be strengthening it. What else is networking, when all is said and done?

I suspect that such considerations weigh heavily in the minds of the French executive elite, for example, who seem even reluctant to leave Paris. But it is also a factor in the attitudes of other European nationalities, in particular the Mediterraneans but even the Germans and, to a lesser extent, the Dutch and the Nordics. Many Europeans show a marked reluctance to cut loose and hand over their destiny to a multinational corporation.

'Cutting loose' is the operative phrase. Geert Hofstede says that "a major problem of expatriates is to obtain the understanding and support of the persons who are not expatriated themselves, but who act as their contacts in the home country organization. The home front should acquire the same cultural sensitivity demanded of the expatriate."

DHL: no room for the Not-Invented-Here

From all outward appearances, one of the most consistently successful companies to mount not just a pan-European but a worldwide operation is the global transport company, DHL Worldwide Express. Since its creation by three California entrepreneurs in 1969, it has spanned the globe via Hong Kong and the Antipodes and literally conquered the world.

Today's DHL is a mature company, but still a private one - most of the founders have moved on and its intermediate owners have ceded two-thirds of their interests to four investors, Lufthansa, Deutsche Post, JAL and Nissho Iwai. This means that outside observers cannot be sure of DHL's profitability despite the appearances, and this may also explain why the company features infrequently in business magazines and books. Yet it must be one of the best examples of how to manage a multinational company with finesse. It continues to enjoy 'uplift', soaring over the wreckage of competitors who had vowed to run it into the ground.

DHL Worldwide Express is an interesting case precisely because it offers a universal product which (1) everybody needs and (2) anybody else could try to emulate. There can be no other reason for its success than its potential to mobilise and manage human beings. The product is the people, delivering on the company's and its clients' promises. And awareness and satisfaction of customer needs, allied with thoughtful human resources management, are the keys to its success.

In its pioneering years, when the company moved into Europe from the Far East, it brought with it a generation of Antipodean managers, Australians and New Zealanders. It is a moot point whether this incidental fact might not have actually helped to conjure up the 'DHL spirit': the cheerful outgoing manner of this generation, fortunately allied with the smell of success, may have helped to overcome the inhibitions and the Not-Invented-Here instincts of native Europeans. It's a thought...

Like many other experienced and successful multinationals, DHL today is a firm believer in, and practitioner of, the 'Think Global, Act Local' approach to international business. "We have learned, from the other aspects of our business, that human resources management has to reflect local market criteria and demands", says Philip Green, DHL's Europe-Africa Chief Operating Officer at its Global Coordination Centre in Brussels. "If experience shows the need to adjust our marketing and customer service policies from country to country, why should HR be any different?"

The operating environment varies significantly from country to country. "It's not just a question of culture," says Guy Colette, DHL's Corporate Affairs Director. "It's also a matter of business habits and of national legislation. With such differences, we have to have accountability at the country level. So each HR manager is responsible for his own territory."

DHL was as conscious as any other multinational of the N-I-H factor in its early years. But the company has developed a number of instruments and procedures to inhibit such thinking. These include global and regional steering groups, including human resources, which meet two or three times a year to provide directional support to 'super-regional' CEOs. Each super-region, Europe for example, has an HR director who provides policy guidance and coordination to country HR managers. The company also encourages cross-fertilisation across frontiers through its 'Best Demonstrated Practice' (BDP) programme. DHL's European management team reflects its multinational mission: two

British directors, one Zimbabwean, one Dutchman, one Belgian and one New Zealander, all reporting to a Dutch CEO.

Equally important is the company's attitude overall to employee motivation. "One of the ways to defuse the N-I-H impulse", says Green, "is to get a lot more people involved in the decision-making process. Much of our effort goes into getting input from country management. They 'buy into' our policies, because they help create them. And the steering groups work both ways. They not only enhance the feedback process, they encourage participants to think in regional and even global terms."

DHL's success ultimately depends on the motivation of its front-line operators - the couriers themselves and the customer service agents. The key to results lies in the ability to ensure their commitment and identification with the company's objectives. "Exposure of our front-line people to what goes on in the company is in direct relation to the quality of communication by their supervisors", says Green. "A priority of our country management is to make them feel that they are close to the global network."

And here may lie one of the secrets of DHL's success. "Whatever promise is made at the origin is, as likely as not, being fulfilled by another DHL team in another country," says Green. "Millions of transactions daily rely on the fact that different parts of the organisation share the same service objectives and contribute equally to customer satisfaction. In this kind of cross-frontier business, there's no room for the Not-Invented-Here...."

Horses for courses?

Before addressing the issue of the EuroLeader, it is worth examining one approach to the whole EuroManager issue which not only has entertainment value, but may encourage the creation of genuinely multicultural teams of EuroManagers **and** provide an incubator environment for future EuroLeaders.

The human resources manager of a multinational company - he happens to be British, which proves a point - publicly risked his opinion some time ago on how the European company of the future might be constituted. He saw the British as team leaders, personnel and operational managers, with the French as the company planners, the Germans as the technicians and engineers, the Scandinavians and Dutch as the middle managers. Sure enough, he picked the Italians as the designers and public relations people.

Other observers endorse many of these opinions. A Parisian lawyer who has made a study of the French business establishment affirms that his country's emphasis on the intellectual side serves research and strategy formulation well, but is less well suited to the flexible responses essential to fast-moving industry.

I have polled over three hundred European managers, consultants and academics of various nationalities on their perception of each nationality's professional strengths and weaknesses. Clearly these perceptions vary according to the observer's standpoint. Even so, certain clusters of opinion emerge.

Very few people challenge the idea that the Germans are the best engineers and technicians, the Italians the best designers and PR people. The Germans (and not the French) get the highest rating on strategic planning - although one could argue that, in today's unstable conditions, this may not be much of a blessing.

The French, in addition to coming second to the Germans in the technical/R+D sphere, get high scores in marketing along with the British, who come tops in financial. Nobody seems to argue with the fact that the Nordics and the Dutch make the best middle managers.

241

Examples of how others do it - No 3

3M Europe: a company of change

"The problem was that, with the old structure, we were duplicating too many resources and were not fast enough in our decision-making processes. There was also the question of where, ultimately, the responsibility for success or failure lay when we marketed a product in Europe. The subsidiaries had a fair degree of autonomy - and still do.

Our business has always been driven by the need to respond rapidly and effectively to customer needs. 3M Europe today operates on a matrix combining product organisations with geographical organisations. With over 50 product divisions not fitting neatly into a common organisational model or industry structure, this is no mean feat!

The product organisations now comprise 10 European Business Centers (EBCs) headquartered at various locations throughout Europe, each of them with its own manufacturing, sales, marketing, logistics and administrative staff and many of them incorporating separate European Business Units (EBUs) for specialised sales and marketing functions. The geographical organisations are our national subsidiaries, grouped in regions. A European Operations Committee coordinates the two and provides financial and human resources management support.

Ours has always been a company of change. The present process was first thought about in 1985 but really got under way in 1992, spurred on by the emergence of the Single Market and changes in the marketplace.

We started out with a fairly clear idea of what we wanted to do. You have to set some principles and models on how to proceed in order to get people to 'buy into' the process. But then you have to get it all to work and you learn as you go along. What you need may differ from one unit to another, depending on the function, the product and so on. The models help you along the road but, when you are dealing with multicultural teams in a fastmoving environment, they are not cast in concrete.

We have a number of factors working for us in implementing this process of change - the underlying philosophy of the company, a tradition of change, mobility within 3M, the fact that many of our managers are long-time employees, and the range of products, markets and issues we are exposed to all the time.

We have to be very sensitive to this question of cultural diversity, just drawing charts won't work. Some people, either because of individual personality or background culture, have to be 'worked on' more than others, you have to listen to them. It helps to know where the person comes from in order to understand them and adopt the right approach."

Stig-Goran Eriksson, Managing Director, 3M France

In view of the limited pedigree of professional German management - a tradition of 30 years at most - it comes as a surprise to find some particularly influential executives in major corporations opting for this nationality for the top management or EuroLeader slot. In fact Germans have been frequently in the news in recent years running the European operations of blue-chip companies like IBM and Xerox, and controlling the global destinies of hi-tech multinationals like Compaq and Apple. The Heidrick & Struggles survey referred to in Chapter 3 concluded that the chance of the "Top 200" companies finding exceptional managers was much higher in Germany than in France.

It seems that they are the exceptions. "German managers still have this tendency to throw their weight and status", says a Danish multinational executive, who believes that the best top EuroManagers must be sourced from the smaller, hence less ethnocentric, countries of Europe. "In the more

The North/South dilemma

A Belgian's view of Nordic management

"The organisational structure is very flat. Decisions are decentralised, and the idea is that every executive/expert consults with his colleagues in order to formulate the right response to a situation.

"It is then put to the President or one of the VPs for the green light. This is purely a formality since, as often as not, the latter will indicate that he is not in a position to make an informed decision. This will probably be evident more from his body language than anything else - at most he will say 'leave it to the experts'...

"You won't find this decision-making process set down anywhere in the management manuals, in the way it would be in an American corporation. It comes quite naturally from the national and organisational cultures.

"The only problem with doing things this way is that decisions take longer to arrive at.

"This kind of distribution of power is quite unthinkable in a Belgian organisation."

conservative German companies, hierarchy and formality can still stop a good idea in its tracks. But there's evidence of an enforced change in the German management culture" he adds, thinking of companies like Bayer and BMW.

Foreigners' perception of those top German executives who have escaped the constraints of their culture is that they are determined, often tough, but even-handed. At the same time, as one British consultant pointed out, "you will often find them operating in a firefighting rather than a visionary mode." For visionaries, look elsewhere.

The same consultant is of the view that the new generation of British managers is as good as you will find anywhere: he describes them as intelligent, able, confident, creative... and hardworking. Another of their own kind says

244

that "the British have changed the most but still have some way to go." And that leaves the question of whether they can operate as well in a multicultural environment.

The problem with the 'horses for courses' idea is that it may encourage the reinforcement of national cultures by functional cultures which, as experience in many large organisations has shown, can be just as potent. Since Germany is essentially an engineering culture, a German engineer will have his cultural prejudices reinforced by his professional predispositions.

Even so - and the thought seemed frivolous when I first entertained it - a selective dosing of cultures, exploiting their natural strengths, could be an intelligent first step to achieving a corporate environment conducive to creating future generations of EuroManagers and EuroLeaders.

Creating a new species

Views on the quality of business school training and its relevance to the needs of the future EuroManager and EuroLeader are very mixed. It is evident that the disillusionment felt by many senior managers with the MBA concept, based on the output of American business schools, has produced a cautious if not cynical attitude towards business education. The curricula of European business schools tend to be more generalist in character and are often tailored for practising managers with some years of work experience. The average age of students at Lausanne's IMD, for example, is 30 compared with a US graduate school average of 26.

Many people agree that a lot more can be done to shape business courses more closely to the demands of the future. Many business school curricula are still 'mechanistic', with the emphasis on operational concerns. This comes at a time when others are telling us that human skills - ranging from cultural sensitivity through team motivation to a proper understanding of how to communicate - will determine failure or success.

A much-travelled American executive active in the communications field says: "I am not aware of any MBA courses in Europe which devote any serious time to PR, public affairs or any other aspect of communications as a main-stream function, apart from one or two optional sessions. We are grooming future CEOs who are ignorant of the importance and the content of the discipline. They don't understand any of the aspects of communications."

Rather to my surprise, a number of respondents also commented very trenchantly, even bitterly, on the human resource function in their companies. It was the one that was singled out most frequently for criticism. Some executives with major corporations dismissed their company's HR department as "useless". The HR director of a very successful mini-multinational concurred: "A lot of personnel managers - for that's the only way to describe them - are too inbred, too immured in the mechanics of their function. They need to have more of the entrepreneurial spirit, understand the realities of business so that they can understand the problems of the people they are responsible for."

It is evident that many major European corporations still fail to appreciate the implications of human resources management in a rapidly changing and multicultural environment. We would do well to look at how others are doing it - large companies that have grown up in a multinational and changing environment, as well as smaller and less hierarchical organisations that have the good fortune not to be culturocentric. Three examples are briefly featured in this chapter. All three have their origins outside Europe.

The process of grooming EuroManagers and EuroLeaders for the business world of the 21st century - characterised by multinationalism in a context of change - will call for as much skill and finesse as any other activity in a corporation. Not enough time and resources are devoted by companies to this vital function.

The first priority is to develop a generation of Euro-HR-Managers equal to the task of creating all-round EuroManagers sharing the same blend of cultural sensitivity and a gift for 'facilitation'.

This will not be easy. In the paper referred to under 'Teamwork' in Chapter 5, Professor Kakabadse and his associates at the Cranfield School of Management comment that, from the results of the School's Top Executive Competency

Research Programme, "exploratory analysis would seem to indicate that there is no general European management style, providing evidence that to 'act European' is at present an unrealistic phenomenon." They indeed identify four distinct styles (page 204) which they define as 'leading from the front' (UK, Ireland, Spain); 'working towards a common goal' (Germany, Austria); 'managing from a distance' (France); and 'consensus' (Sweden, Finland, Ireland).

At the same time, Kakabadse insists, "there is no secret to running a successful business. There is no one country or culture better adjusted or more naturally gifted than any other to the effective management of an enterprise. To differing degrees, the same sorts of problems are shared across different nation states. The skill is not to be blinded by national parochial differences."

In fact, precisely because of this, some people think the simplest solution is to choose a non-European to head a pan-European team! There is some evidence that people from other parts of the world can exploit the absence of a intra-European cultural bias, real or perceived, to good effect. This particularly applies to Americans, if they manage to tune their cultural attenae (and, with some very impressive exceptions, many of them have difficulty doing so).

One of the hopes must obviously be that the opening up of frontiers and efforts to educate young people as 'world citizens' will combine to create future generations free of the cultural constraints of their predecessors. This can only be a hope, as there are few signs yet that the differences are wearing thin. Hofstede even states quite categorically in his book *Cultures and Organizations* that "there is no evidence that the cultures of present-day generations from different countries are converging."

So where do we go from here?

Human skills, especially the ability to understand and motivate people of widely ranging cultures and backgrounds, will be the EuroManager's trump card. I discussed the options with Baldwin Klep who, as an international executive search consultant with Heidrick & Struggles, spends his time recruiting people for EuroLeader-type jobs.

"My definition of a EuroManager - what you call a EuroLeader - is someone who has bottom-line responsibility for a range of products or services across part or all of Europe." This corresponds with the role of the Managing Directors of 3M's European Business Centers (see page 242).

The tools of the international manager's trade

Two-way communication: the ability to engage in meaningful dialogue rather than lecturing to individuals from the foreign culture.

Empathy: the ability to see a situation from the other person's perspective.

Respect for host-country nationals: the ability to communicate esteem for persons from other cultures.

Ability to be subjective, personalising one's knowledge and perception without being judgemental.

Openness: willingness to share aspects of one's personal life with members of a foreign culture.

Integration of task and relationship dimensions of the job, i.e learning to be relation-oriented as well as task-oriented (NB: the authors of this study are Canadian).

Tolerance for ambiguity: the ability to live and work effectively in unclear cross-cultural situations.

Goal-directed persistence in the face of setbacks: the ability to continue to work toward a desired goal in the face of setbacks, also to approach goal attainment from an 'equifinality' perspective, i.e. there is more than one way to reach a goal.

plus, of course, the appropriate professional competences!

Source: Rubin, B.D.; Askling, L.R.; and Kealey, D.J.
Cross-cultural Effectiveness: an Overview.

"He or she has to be a change-maker, someone who is not intimidated by the *status quo* and can take the initiative in changing both structures and mentalities. In addition, he or she has to have proven multicultural effectiveness which, among other things, means exercising a great deal of diplomacy. The problem in finding the right people for this kind of job is that line managers and diplomacy don't always mix!"

"But you need to build the trust that is so often lacking when a multicultural team comes together for the first time. As Europeans, we don't know each other well enough, which means that we start out from a standpoint of suspicion. So we have to create the trust and then initiate change in a transparent way - so that everyone 'buys in' to the process. The EuroManager is in effect a facilitator, understanding and working with people, involving them in the process of change."

"The British have precisely these qualities. It's my impression, and others say the same thing, that the biggest resource of potential EuroManagers is to be found among British people now working for multinationals." The younger generation of Britons in particular are good people managers, at ease in teamwork, increasingly professional and hardworking. But they first have to break out of the shell of their insularity, just as the Germans have to moderate their single-mindedness and mania for specialisation, and the French their penchant for elitism and autocracy.

So how does one become a EuroManager?

"It starts with birth and goes on through your formative years - some people are more predisposed to a multicultural environment than others. If you're one of them, then ideally you go to a foreign university followed, maybe, by a stint working not in Europe but in a relatively 'neutral' culture like the US. This helps give you objectivity, even towards your own culture. If you can follow this up by working and living in a number of international situations, so much the better."

"This is all background. How you actually prove yourself as a EuroManager depends on the challenge. First, you have to understand the structure of your organisation and decide what improvements can be made: many European companies still have an 'export' mentality at a time when the Single European Market has become a reality, and many of them still have ethnocentric headquarters operations."

"Second, you have to understand the market. Keep the decision-making as close to the customer as you can. European markets are coming closer together, but they still have their idiosyncracies."

"And, finally, give 'added value'. You have to be a **manager**, empowering people in the process, and not just a coordinator. Coordinators don't add value."

A challenge to one's powers of imagination? Maybe. But then it may still be easier to believe in EuroManagers than in little green men...

ABB and the ABC of multicultural management

Enough years - to be precise, four - have passed since the original edition of this book to give me time both to reflect on what I have said and to observe the continuing practice of multicultural management. My main conclusion is that, on the evidence of companies like the giant ABB and the relatively puny but dynamic AspenTech (see pages 236/7), the 'Think Global, Act Local' approach is as good as any other nostrum on offer.

I used to feel it was a bit of a cop-out, a soft option, but in the absence of anything more radical - culture-free clones for example (god help us!) - it has a lot going for it. Provided strict measures are taken to avoid the propagation of the Not-Invented-Here syndrome, it may indeed foster the kind of environment that will eventually spawn a breed of EuroManagers.

ABB, the product of the merger between Sweden's ASEA and Switzerland's Brown Boveri, firmly nailed the 'Think Global, Act Local' banner to its masthead in the formative years under the leadership of Percy Barnevik. The resulting organisation, which now employs over 200,000 people worldwide, operates on the principle of what Barnevik called, in an interview with *The Wall Street Journal*, "multi-domestic decentralisation".

By the time Barnevik left ABB in 1987 to head up the Wallenberg family's Investor holding, the implementation phase of the merger was complete. "In most successful cross-frontier mergers," comments his successor, Göran Lindahl, "the implementation process has to be fast. You cannot afford to dither."

ABB operates a matrix system under which responsibilities - and accountabilities - devolve to the level of some 5,000 profit centres within a total of over 1,000 companies. A typical profit centre will employ 40-50 people, giving a compact team that both moves fast and keeps close to its customers. "This combination of decentralisation and small profit centres also helps create an 'incubator environment' in which we are able to give early responsibility to promising young managers", comments Hans-Henning Quast, ABB Europe's VP of Human Resources.

Far from imposing a style or culture overall, ABB holds the corporate circle by practising enlightened decentralisation with a small but effective central management cadre. Head office staff numbers have fallen from 4,000 in 1988 to 150 today. These include the senior executive team in Zurich which comprises President and CEO Lindahl and seven VPs, representing four nationalities: German, Swedish, Swiss and American.

"Our whole cultural thinking is to be at home everywhere, not looking at the world from one epicentre", comments Eberhard von Koerber, President of ABB Europe in Brussels. "Our company managers in Italy are Italian and in Austria, Austrian. Our competitors have their Germans or their Americans sitting there. We're closer to the customer."

Closeness to the customer, in terms of both geographical proximity and shared identity, is important in most of ABB's business segments, many of which are selling to state-owned organisations or strategic industries. At the same time many of these customer organisations are active internationally and many of ABB's skills, services and products are sourced globally. Through this intricate matrix of interests, ABB

251

manages to reconcile the tension between the Global and the Local.

ABB is committed to developing people locally for the key national jobs, "even to the level of chief financial officer" says Quast. These national units are supported by a team of global expatriates - what von Koerber calls "rapid deployment forces... skinny, sporty, long-distance runner types, mid-thirties, resistant to the temptations of loneliness and wilderness, go-getters who like the smell of powder..."

Improved cooperation between nationalities and heightened cross-cultural awareness and sensitivity are long-term priorities for ABB. Projects now underway around the world in support of these objectives include a European short-term assignment programme currently involving some 300 executives yearly, most of them operational managers.

"This is not an arbitrary process imposed from above, nor does ABB Corporate finance it", comments Hans-Henning Quast. "It reflects real-time operating company needs. If our Polish company wants to gain knowhow on a particular aspect of CAD/CAM design or inventory control, we look for the most qualified person in our organisation. Availability permitting, he or she then goes on short-time assignment - between three and twelve months maximum - without being uprooted from the home environment.

"Naturally enough", continues Quast, "while the host company benefits from the knowhow, both sides benefit from the improvement in cultural understanding." Costs are shared on a negotiated basis by the companies involved to reflect the reality of the situation ("the learner pays more than the teacher"), but there is often an element of mutual interest. One of the by-products is cross-fertilisation, another is the brainstorming potential such opportunities provide.

Certainly ABB's pioneering work - in moving over the years from corporate colonialism to the successful merger of two major companies of distinctly different cultures - offers hope to others contemplating a dive into the murky waters of multinationalism. Maybe the EuroManager will be rendered redundant as the Global Manager takes over...?

BIBLIOGRAPHY

1   Hill, Richard. *WeEuropeans*.
    Brussels: Europublic, 1997.

2   Hofstede, Geert. *Cultures and Organizations*.
    London: McGraw-Hill Book Company, 1991.

3   Hoppe, M H. *A Comparative Study of Country Elites:
    International Differences in Work-related Values and
    Learning and their Implications for Management
    Training and Development*. Unpublished Ph.D. Thesis.
    University of North Carolina at Chapel Hill.

4   Hall, Edward T. *Beyond Culture*.
    New York: Anchor Books/Doubleday, 1976.

5   Barzini, Luigi. *The Europeans*.
    London: Penguin, 1983.

6   Messmer, Max. *Staffing Europe*. Herndon,
    VA: Acropolis Books, 1992.

7   McNeil, W H. *The Metamorphosis of Greece since
    World War II*.
    Chicago: University of Chicago, 1978.

8   Habert, Kjell and Lillebø, Arild. *Made in Norway -
    Norwegians as others see them*.
    Oslo: Alicom Publishing, 1992.

9   Barsoux, Jean-Louis and Lawrence, Peter.
    Management in France.
    London: Cassell, 1990.

10 Zeldin, Theodore. *The French*.
    London: Collins Harvill, 1983.

11 Ardagh, John. *Germany and the Germans*.
    London: Penguin, 1990.

12 Humes, Samuel. *Managing the Multinational*.
    London: Prentice Hall, 1993.

13 Marsh, David. *The Germans*.
    London: Century Hutchinson, 1989.

14 Glouchevitch, Philip. *Juggernaut: The Keys to
    German Business Success*.
    New York: Touchstone, 1993.

15   Stroebe, Wolfgang. *Is Social Psychology really that complicated?*.
     European Journal of Social Psychology, **6**, 4.

16   Kakabadse, A. *The Success Levers for Europe: The Cranfield Executive Competences Survey*. Bradford: MCB University Press, The Journal of Management Development, **12**, 8.

17   Crozier, Michel. *Strategies for Change: The Future of French Society*.
     Massachusetts: MIT Press, 1982.

18   Ardagh, John. *France in the 1980s: The Definitive Book*. Harmondsworth,
     U.K.: Penguin, 1982.

19   Mole, John. *Mind your Manners*.
     London: The Industrial Society, 1990.

20   Frischer, Dominique. *La France vue d'en Face*.
     Paris: Robert Laffont, 1990.

21   Horovitz, Jacques Henri. *Top Management Control in Europe*.
     London: Macmillan, 1980.

22   Barzini, Luigi. *The Italians*.
     New York: Atheneum, 1964.

23   Miller, Stuart. *Painted in Blood*.
     New York: Atheneum, 1987.

24   Diaz-Plaja, Fernando. *El Espanol y los Siete Pecados Capitales*.
     Madrid: Alianza Editorial, 1970.

25   Ames, Helen Wattley. *Spain is Different*.
     Yarmouth (Maine): Intercultural Press, 1992.

26   de Madariaga, Salvador. *Spain*.
     London: Jonathan Cape, 1942.

27   Brenan, Gerald. *The Face of Spain*.
     London: Penguin, 1965.

28   Schama, Simon. *The Embarrassment of Riches*.
     London: William Collins, 1987.

29   Granick, David. *The European Executive*.
     New York: Doubleday, 1962.

30   Phillips-Martinsson, Jean. *Swedes as Others see Them.*
      Lund: Studentlitteratur, 1991.

31   Kakabadse, A; Myers, A; Okazaki-Ward, L. *The Top
      Executive Competency Research Programme:
      European Analysis with Special Emphasis on Finland.*
      Helsinki: LIFIM Bulletin, Finnish Institute of
      Management, 1993.

32   d'Iribarne, Philippe. *La logique de l'honneur: Gestion
      des entreprises et traditions nationales.*
      Paris: Editions du Seuil, 1989.

33   Shetter, William Z. *The Netherlands in Perspective.*
      Leiden: Martinus Nijhoff, 1987.

34   Mead, Richard. *Cross-Cultural Management
      Communication.*
      Chichester (UK): John Wiley, 1990.

35   Fisher, Glen. *International Negotiation.*
      Yarmouth (Maine): Intercultural Press, 1980.

36   Salacuse, Jeswald W. *Making Global Deals.*
      New York/Toronto: Times Books, 1991.

37   Collett, Peter. *Foreign Bodies.*
      London, Simon & Schuster, 1993.

38   de Urbina, José Antonio.
      El Protocolo en los Negocios.
      Madrid: Temas de Hoy, 1994.

39   Posses, F. *The Art of International Negotiations.*
      London: Business Books, 1978.

40   Campbell, Nigel C G; Graham, John L; Jolibert, Alain;
      Meissner, Hans Gunther. *Marketing Negotiations in
      France, Germany, the United Kingdom, and the United
      States.* Journal of Marketing, **52** (April 1988).

41   Handy, Charles. *Age of Paradox.*
      Boston: Harvard Business, 1994.

42   Hammer, Michael and Champy, James. *Reengineering
      the Corporation: A Manifesto for Business Revolution.*
      London: Nicolas Brealey, 1993

INDEX

261